Unlocking Your Great Potential Within You:
Using the Superpowers of Meditation
Executive Functioning Skills
Good Habits
We Can Do It!

Illustrator
@alamins_design_hub
@alamins_world

Alisa L. Grace

Unlocking Your Great Potential Within You:

Using the Superpowers of

Meditation

Executive Functioning Skills

Good Habits

We Can Do It!

© 2024 Alisa L. Grace

All rights reserved.

No part of this book may be reproduced in any form or by any electronic or mechanical means, including information storage and retrieval systems, without permission in writing from the publisher.

Self-Published by
Alisa L. Grace
Sanford, FL 32771

ISBN: 978-1-966129-68-4

First Edition

Printed in the United States of America

Library of Congress Cataloging-in-Publication Data
Grace, Alisa L.
Title of the Book: Unlocking Your Great Potential Within You: The Super Natural Powers of Meditation, Executive Functioning Skills, and Good Habits We Can Do It
Library of Congress Control Number: 2025901753

Disclaimer: The views expressed in this book are those of the author and do not necessarily reflect any organizations or individuals mentioned.

Acknowledgments: The author wishes to thank God, Her Husband (Linion), Victory Temple of God, Florida SPECS, Unity Youth Association, All About Serving You, Angels-ANJ Events, NordeVest, and Love & Create Life for their support and contributions.

This book is dedicated to:

To my dearly beloved Heavenly Father, I am honored you chose me for this task. You have been with me through the entire process, guiding and leading me.

To all students with disabilities and teachers of these precious students: you are unique for a reason. Embrace it and become who you have been designed to be.

To Orange and Seminole County Public School Systems, who provided me with the teaching, training, and opportunity to apply what I have been taught/trained to teach, coach academically, and supervise as an administrator. I am forever grateful to both countries.

To the ESE Teachers who teach our students with disabilities. This curriculum will help you as you continue to serve and support the students who require extended support.

For these are all our children, we will either profit from or pay for whatever they become.

James Baldwin

Introduction to the Curriculum:

Unlocking Your Great Potential Within You Using the Superpowers of Meditation, Executive Functioning Skills, and Good Habits

Dear Students,

Welcome to the *"Unlocking Your Great Potential"* curriculum! This workbook is your guide to an exciting journey of self-discovery, personal growth, and success. You will learn how to unlock your unique strengths and talents while overcoming challenges through engaging stories, meaningful activities, and practical tools.

This curriculum is designed with **you** in mind. It was created to reflect real-life experiences and challenges you might face at school, home, or in your personal life. Each story and activity is crafted to inspire you and help you develop powerful skills like meditation, goal setting, organization, and building good habits.

Here's what you can expect:

- **Explore Who You Are:** You will begin by discovering what makes you unique, celebrating your individuality, and understanding how your strengths can help you overcome challenges.
- **Learn Essential Skills:** From calming your mind with meditation to organizing your tasks with executive functioning skills, you'll gain tools to make your life easier and more successful.
- **Set Goals and Take Action:** You will learn how to set meaningful goals, create action plans, and reflect on your progress to stay on track and motivated.
- **Build Good Habits:** Developing positive routines and habits will help you perform better in school and lead a happier, healthier life.

This curriculum is written **for you and about you**. These stories' characters are students like you, navigating similar situations and challenges. Their experiences are designed to resonate with you, giving you a voice and showing you that you are not alone.

We want you to know that it's okay to be different, to learn differently, and to take your own unique path. This program celebrates your individuality and empowers you to thrive in ways that are meaningful to you.

A Message of Encouragement

Remember, you are capable of amazing things! This workbook is your tool for unlocking the greatness that already exists within you. As you complete each activity and reflect on each lesson, you will take steps toward becoming your best version.

We are so proud of you for taking this journey, and we are cheering you on every step of the way. Let's get started and unlock your great potential together!

You've got this! ✮

With excitement and belief in you,

Alisa L. Grace
Author

How to Use this Workbook:

Unlocking Your Great Potential Within You Using the Superpowers of Meditation, Executive Functioning Skills, and Good Habits

Dear Students,

This workbook is your personal guide to unlocking your great potential! Inside, you'll find stories, activities, and tools designed to help you discover who you are, develop essential skills, and achieve your goals. Here's how to make the most of it:

1. Start Each Unit with an Open Mind

Each unit begins with a story featuring relatable characters who are navigating challenges and learning valuable lessons—just like you! Read these stories carefully, and consider how they connect to your life.

2. Reflect and Participate in Activities

After each story, you'll find activities that encourage you to reflect on what you've learned and apply it to your own experiences. These activities are designed to:

- Help you identify your strengths and challenges.
- Teach you new skills like meditation, goal setting, and time management.
- Inspire you to create positive habits and routines.

Take your time with each activity and answer honestly. This is your space to grow!

3. Set Goals and Create Action Plans

Throughout this workbook, you'll set personal and academic goals. You'll learn how to break them down into steps and track your progress. Use these tools to stay focused and motivated as you work toward success.

---

4. Engage in Reflection and Growth

At the end of each unit, you'll find reflection questions that help you look back on what you've learned and how you've grown. Take these moments seriously—they are your chance to celebrate your progress and plan your next steps.

---

5. Work Together and Support Each Other

You're not on this journey alone! Many activities involve sharing and collaborating with your classmates. Encourage each other, listen to one another, and share ideas. Together, you'll build a supportive community where everyone feels valued.

---

6. Ask for Help When Needed

Your teacher is here to guide and support you. Don't hesitate to ask for assistance if you're unsure about an activity or need help with a concept. This workbook is about helping you succeed, and your teacher is here to help you every step of the way.

---

7. Celebrate Your Achievements

As you work through this workbook, remember to celebrate every step of progress you make. Every reflection, every goal achieved, and every skill learned is a win!

---

8. Unlock Your Great Potential!

This workbook is a powerful tool for helping you become the best version of yourself. Take it seriously, put in the effort, and trust the process. You'll be amazed at what you can achieve when you unleash your unique strengths and embrace who you are.

Let's get started and unlock the greatness within you!

You've got this, and we're here to cheer you on! 🎉

Alisa L. Grace
Author

Table of Contents

Letter to Students 17
Unlocking Your Great Potential! 19
Unit 1: I Am Unique: Discovering Who I Am and Unleashing My Powers (Weeks 1-4) 21
Week 1: Understanding Uniqueness 25
Week 2: Celebrating Individuality 38
Week 3: Self-Reflection and Goal Setting 47
Week 4: Unleashing My Powers 56
Unit 2: The Superpower of Meditation (Weeks 5-9) 65
Week 5: The Basics of Meditation 69
Week 6: Building a Meditation Practice 78
Week 7: Applying Meditation to Daily Life 87
Week 8: Advanced Meditation Techniques 96
Week 9: Integrating Meditation with Learning 105
Unit 3: The Superpower of Executive Functioning Skills (Weeks 10-15) 117
Week 10: Introduction to Executive Functioning 119
Week 11: Developing Planning and Organization Skills 129
Week 12: Enhancing Memory and Focus 138
Week 13: Problem-Solving and Flexibility 145
Week 14: Enhancing Self-Monitoring and Task Initiation 152
Week 15: Integrating Executive Functioning with Academics 159
Unit 4: The Superpower of Good Habits (Weeks 16-21) 167
Week 16: Understanding Habits 169
Week 17: Building Positive Habits 175
Week 18: Replacing Negative Habits 180
Week 19: Developing Consistency 186
Week 20: Habitual Growth and Adaptation 192

Week 21: Integrating Good Habits with Academics 198

Unit 5: Superpowers to Academics **205**
Week 22: Reading Strategies 208
Week 23: Reading Strategies Continued 214
Week 24: Math Strategies 220
Week 25: Math Strategies Continued 226
Week 26: Science Strategies 232
Week 27: Science Strategies Continued 238

Unit 6: Applying Superpowers to Social Skills and Conflict Resolution **245**
Week 28: Social Skills 248
Week 29: Social Skills Continued 254
Week 30: Conflict Resolution 260
Week 31: Conflict Resolution Continued 266
Week 32: Integrating Social Skills and Conflict Resolution 272
Week 33: Reflection and Growth 278

Unit 7: Putting It All Together **283**
Week 34: Combing Superpowers 286
Week 35: Practical Application 292

Unit 8: Maintaining and Sustaining Growth **299**
Week 36: Sustaining Practices 302

Tab 1: Surveys **309**
Additional Resources **331**
Meet the Author **333**

Letter to Students

Dear Students,

I am thrilled to introduce you to our new curriculum, "Unlocking Your Great Potential." This program has been specially designed with you in mind, aiming to help you recognize and unleash your unique strengths and abilities. The stories and activities you will encounter are crafted from an understanding and empathetic perspective, featuring classroom settings and characters that you will find relatable and inspiring.

Understanding and Empathy

Being a student can come with many challenges, especially when you genuinely need help understanding your experiences and concerns. This curriculum is different. It is written to give you a voice that is heard and valued. Each story and activity has been created to reflect the real-life situations and emotions that you might face, showing that you are not alone in your journey.

Your Voice Matters

In this curriculum, your voice is not only heard but celebrated. The stories include characters like you, facing similar challenges and triumphs, making their way through school and life just as you are. We address issues that may have been overlooked or misunderstood, ensuring your concerns and feelings are acknowledged and respected.

Addressing Your Concerns

We understand that you have dealt with various issues that might have seemed invisible to others. This curriculum aims to address those very concerns with empathy and practical strategies. From managing stress and developing good habits to setting goals and celebrating your individuality, every part of this curriculum is designed to support you in ways that truly matter.

Cheering You On

As you embark on this journey with us, know that we are cheering you on every step of the way. We believe in your potential and are committed to helping you unlock the greatness within you. Through the stories, activities, and lessons, you will discover your unique powers and learn how to use them to succeed in school, at home, and in your personal life.

Remember, you are unique, and your individuality is your greatest strength. Embrace who you are and work together to unlock your full potential. Get ready to blow us away with all the fantastic things you will accomplish! Here's to your journey of self-discovery and growth!

With enthusiasm and support,

Alisa L. Grace

Unlocking Your Great Potential!

Unit 1: I Am Unique

Discovering Who I Am and Unleashing My Powers (Weeks 1-4)

Introduction to Unit 1: I Am Unique - Discovering Who I Am and Unleashing My Powers

Strategy Middle/High School

Welcome, Strategy Middle/High School students, to the beginning of a transformative journey through Unit 1: "I Am Unique - Discovering Who I Am and Unleashing My Powers." Over the next four weeks, we will explore the importance of understanding and embracing your unique strengths and challenges. By knowing who you are and celebrating your individuality, you can unlock your full potential and perform to the best of your ability.

Week 1: Understanding Uniqueness

Our first week will focus on understanding what makes us unique. Everyone has different talents, interests, and ways of learning. By recognizing and appreciating these differences, you can see how your unique qualities contribute to your success. It's important to remember that being different is not a disadvantage—it's your superpower!

Week 2: Celebrating Individuality

During the second week, we will celebrate our individuality. You will learn how to embrace your strengths and work with your challenges. We will share our unique qualities, creating a supportive community where everyone feels valued and understood. Celebrating who you are helps build confidence and encourages you to use your strengths to achieve your goals.

Week 3: Self-Reflection and Goal Setting

In the third week, we will dive into self-reflection and goal setting. Understanding your strengths and challenges is the first step; setting realistic and achievable goals is the next. By reflecting on your experiences and setting clear goals, you can create a roadmap to success. We will also discuss strategies for staying motivated and tracking your progress.

Week 4: Unleashing My Powers

In the final week of this unit, we will introduce you to three powerful tools: meditation, executive functioning skills, and good habits. These skills will help you manage stress, stay organized, and develop positive routines. Integrating these practices into daily life can improve focus, productivity, and overall well-being.

The Importance of Knowing and Embracing Your Uniqueness

For students with disabilities, understanding and accepting that you are different and learn differently is crucial. Here's why:

1. **Self-Awareness:** Knowing your strengths and challenges allows you to leverage your abilities and seek help when needed. It helps you advocate for yourself and communicate your needs effectively.

2. **Confidence:** Embracing your uniqueness builds self-confidence. When you understand that being different is not a limitation but a unique perspective, you can approach challenges with a positive mindset.

3. **Resilience:** Accepting that learning differently is okay helps you develop resilience. You learn to adapt and find strategies that work for you, which is essential for overcoming obstacles.

4. **Personal Growth:** By recognizing and working with your unique qualities, you can set and achieve individual goals, leading to continuous growth and improvement.

5. **Supportive Community:** Sharing your experiences and learning from others creates a supportive environment where everyone feels valued. You are not alone in your journey; others understand and can offer support.

As we embark on this journey through Unit 1, remember that you are unique, and your individuality is your greatest strength. We will explore, celebrate, and unleash your powers together, setting the foundation for a successful and fulfilling school year.

Let's begin this exciting journey of self-discovery and growth!

Welcome to "I Am Unique: Discovering Who I Am and Unleashing My Powers!"

Week 1:
Understanding Uniqueness

Lesson 1: Introduction to the Curriculum

Lesson 1: Introduction to the Curriculum

Conduct PreSurvy for Unit 1

Read This Story to Introduce the Curriculum:

Introduction Story: Unlocking Your Great Potential Within You

---

Characters:

- **Kenlyn:** A creative artist who finds staying calm and managing stress challenging.
- **Nyrie:** An avid reader who sometimes struggles with reading comprehension and focus.
- **Ahlani:** A curious student with a passion for history, but needs help to stay organized.
- **Nia:** Is a social butterfly who wants to improve her communication skills and time management.
- **Lenny:** A science enthusiast who often feels overwhelmed by complex experiments.
- **Noah:** A budding inventor who struggles with maintaining focus and organization.
- **Na'ima:** A math lover who needs help developing consistent study habits.
- **Naudia:** An empathetic student who wants to improve her conflict resolution skills.
- **Mason:** A student with a music talent but has difficulty managing stress and anxiety.
- **Kimiyah:** A determined learner who needs support with executive functioning skills.
- **Levi:** A tech-savvy student who wants to enhance his problem-solving skills.
- **Nilan:** A sports enthusiast who needs to work on planning and organization.
- **Mrs. Grace:** The compassionate and supportive learning strategies teacher.

Strategies Middle and High School's new and exciting program was about to begin. Mrs. Grace, the dedicated learning strategies teacher, welcomed her students to an empowering class designed to help them unlock their great potential. The students, Kenlyn, Nyrie, Ahlani,

Nia, Lenny, Noah, Na'ima, Naudia, Mason, Kimiyah, Levi, and Nilan, all had unique talents and faced different challenges in their learning journeys.

Mrs. Grace: "Welcome, everyone! This year, we're embarking on a transformative journey with our new curriculum, 'Unlocking Your Great Potential Within You.' This program is designed to help you discover and unleash your unique strengths using the superpowers of meditation, executive functioning skills, and good habits."

The students listened attentively, curious about how this curriculum would help them overcome their challenges.

Kenlyn: "How can meditation help me manage my stress and stay calm?"

Mrs. Grace: "Great question, Kenlyn! Meditation will teach you mindfulness and relaxation techniques that can reduce stress and help you stay focused. This will enhance your creativity and allow you to express yourself better in art."

Nyrie: "I love reading, but sometimes I struggle to understand and remember what I read. Will this program help me?"

Mrs. Grace: "Absolutely, Nyrie! We'll use meditation to improve your concentration and executive functioning skills to help you organize your thoughts. You'll also learn good habits to improve your reading practice."

Ahlani: "I have so much curiosity about history, but I find it hard to stay organized with my notes and assignments."

Mrs. Grace: "Ahlani, you'll learn executive functioning skills like planning and organization, which will help you keep track of your notes and assignments. This will make studying history more enjoyable and productive for you."

Nia: "I love talking to people, but I want to improve my communication skills and manage my time better."

Mrs. Grace: "Nia, through this curriculum, you'll develop better communication skills and learn to manage your time effectively. This will help you build stronger relationships and balance your social life with your studies."

Lenny: "I get excited about science, but sometimes the experiments feel overwhelming."

Mrs. Grace: "Lenny, meditation will help you stay calm and focused during experiments, and executive functioning skills will help you break down complex tasks into manageable steps."

Noah: "I want to be an inventor but struggle with focus and organization."

Mrs. Grace: "Noah, this program will help you develop the focus and organizational skills you need to bring your inventions to life. Meditation will enhance your concentration, and good habits will keep you on track."

Na'ima: "I love math but need help with consistent study habits."

Mrs. Grace: "Na'ima, you'll learn how to build and maintain good habits that will support your love for math and make studying more effective."

Naudia: "I want to help others and improve my conflict resolution skills."

Mrs. Grace: "Naudia, you'll learn techniques for resolving conflicts peacefully and empathetically, making you a better friend and leader."

Mason: "I get anxious sometimes, especially before performing music."

Mrs. Grace: "Mason, meditation will help you manage your anxiety and build confidence, allowing you to perform at your best."

Kimiyah: "I want to improve my executive functioning skills to stay on top of my schoolwork."

Mrs. Grace: "Kimiyah, you'll learn valuable skills like planning, organization, and time management to help you excel in your studies."

Levi: "I love technology and problem-solving but want to improve."

Mrs. Grace: "Levi, this curriculum will enhance your problem-solving skills and help you apply them more effectively to your tech projects."

Nilan: "I need help planning and organizing, especially with my sports activities."

Mrs. Grace: "Nilan, you'll learn to plan better and organize your time, balancing your sports and academic responsibilities."

Mrs. Grace smiled at her students, filled with confidence in their potential. "Together, we will unlock your great potential within you. This curriculum is not just about academics; it's about empowering you to succeed at home, school, and community. Let's embark on this journey and discover the amazing things you can achieve!"

The students felt a sense of excitement and determination. They were ready to unlock their superpowers and embark on a transformative journey with Mrs. Grace leading the way.

Lesson 2:
I Am Unique

Lesson 2:
I Am Unique

Read Story:

Story: I Am Unique

At Strategies Middle and High School, the bell rang to signal the start of Mrs. Grace's learning strategies class. The students, each with unique talents and challenges, filed into the room and took their seats. Today, Mrs. Grace had something special planned to help her students understand and embrace their differences.

Mrs. Grace began the class with a warm smile. "Good morning, everyone! Today, we will talk about what makes each of us unique. We all have different strengths and challenges, and that's something to celebrate."

She handed out colorful sheets of paper and markers to each student. "I want you to draw or write about one thing that makes you unique. It can be a talent, a hobby, or something you love doing."

The classroom buzzed with activity as the students began to express their uniqueness. After a few minutes, Mrs. Grace asked them to share their creations.

Kenlyn was the first to speak. "I drew a paintbrush because I love painting. It helps me express my feelings, even though I sometimes get stressed about my work."

Next, Nyrie shared his piece. "I wrote about how much I love reading. Books take me to different worlds, but I sometimes struggle to focus and understand everything."

Ahlani held up her drawing. "I have a magnifying glass because I'm curious about history. I love learning about the past but struggle to organize my notes and assignments."

Nia followed with her illustration. "I drew a group of friends because I love being around people. I want to improve my communication skills and manage my time better to balance my social life and schoolwork."

Lenny showed his work next. "I have a drawing of a science experiment. I love science, but the experiments can be overwhelming for me."

Noah shared his creation with pride. "I wrote about my inventions. I love creating new things but have trouble staying focused and organized."

Na'ima held up her paper. "I drew a math book because I love solving math problems, but I need help developing good study habits."

Naudia's drawing was a heart. "I have a heart because I care about others and want to help people. I want to improve my conflict resolution skills to make a bigger difference."

Mason's artwork featured a guitar. "I drew a guitar because music is my passion. I get anxious before performing and need help managing my stress."

Kimiyah shared her determination through words. "I wrote about my determination to learn. I need support with executive functioning skills to stay on top of my schoolwork."

Levi held up his drawing of a computer. "I have a computer because I love technology. I want to get better at problem-solving."

Finally, Nilan displayed his drawing. "I drew a soccer ball because I love sports. I need to work on better planning and organizing my time."

Mrs. Grace smiled as she looked at the colorful display of uniqueness. "Look at all these amazing strengths and interests! Each of you brings something special to our class. It's important to remember that we all learn and process information differently. That's what makes us unique."

She pointed to a poster on the wall that read, "Embrace Your Differences."

"Our differences are our strengths," she continued. "They make us who we are. This class will teach us to use our unique abilities to overcome challenges. We'll support each other and celebrate our progress together."

The students nodded, feeling a sense of pride and belonging. They understood that being different was something to be proud of and that their unique ways of learning were valuable.

Mrs. Grace concluded, "Remember, you are all unique, which makes you special. Embrace your differences and work together to unlock your great potential."

The students left the class with renewed confidence, ready to face challenges and celebrate their strengths, knowing that their uniqueness was their superpower.

Lesson 3: Identifying Personal Strengths and Challenges

Lesson 3:
Identifying Personal Strengths and Challenges

Story: Understanding Uniqueness - Identifying Personal Strengths and Challenges

---

At Strategy Middle and High School, Mrs. Grace's learning strategies class was buzzing with excitement. Today, she had planned a special lesson to help her students understand their unique strengths and challenges. The class was a mix of students, each with their own talents and difficulties, and Mrs. Grace knew how important it was for them to recognize and embrace their individuality.

The students gathered in a circle, their colorful papers and markers ready. Mrs. Grace began the lesson with a warm smile.

"Good morning, everyone! Today, we're going to explore what makes each of us unique. We all have different strengths and challenges, and it's important to understand and appreciate these differences."

She handed out colorful sheets of paper and markers to each student. "I want you to draw or write about one thing that makes you unique. It can be a talent, a hobby, or something you love doing."

The classroom buzzed with activity as the students began to express their uniqueness. After a few minutes, Mrs. Grace asked them to share their creations.

Kenlyn, a creative artist, was the first to speak. "I drew a paintbrush because I love painting. It helps me express my feelings, even though I sometimes get stressed about my work."

Next, Nyrie shared his piece. "I wrote about how much I love reading. Books take me to different worlds, but I sometimes struggle to focus and understand everything."

Ahlani held up her drawing. "I have a magnifying glass because I'm curious about history. I love learning about the past but struggle to organize my notes and assignments."

Nia followed with her illustration. "I drew a group of friends because I love being around people. I want to improve my communication skills and manage my time better to balance my social life and schoolwork."

Lenny showed his work next. "I have a drawing of a science experiment. I love science, but the experiments can be overwhelming for me."

Noah shared his creation with pride. "I wrote about my inventions. I love creating new things but have trouble staying focused and organized."

Na'ima held up her paper. "I drew a math book because I love solving math problems, but I need help developing good study habits."

Naudia's drawing was a heart. "I have a heart because I care about others and want to help people. I want to improve my conflict resolution skills to make a bigger difference."

Mason's artwork featured a guitar. "I drew a guitar because music is my passion. I get anxious before performing and need help managing my stress."

Kimiyah shared her determination through words. "I wrote about my determination to learn. I need support with executive functioning skills to stay on top of my schoolwork."

Levi held up his drawing of a computer. "I have a computer because I love technology. I want to get better at problem-solving."

Finally, Nilan displayed his drawing. "I drew a soccer ball because I love sports. I need to work on better planning and organizing my time."

Mrs. Grace smiled as she looked at the colorful display of uniqueness. "Look at all these amazing strengths and interests! Each of you brings something special to our class. It's important to remember that we all learn and process information differently. That's what makes us unique."

She pointed to a poster on the wall that read, "Embrace Your Differences."

"Our differences are our strengths," she continued. "They make us who we are. This class will teach us to use our unique abilities to overcome challenges. We'll support each other and celebrate our progress together."

The students nodded, feeling a sense of pride and belonging. They understood that being different was something to be proud of and that their unique ways of learning were valuable.

Mrs. Grace concluded, "Remember, you are all unique, which makes you special. Embrace your differences and work together to unlock your great potential."

As the students left the class, they had renewed confidence, ready to face challenges and celebrate their strengths. They knew their uniqueness was their superpower, and with Mrs. Grace's guidance, they were excited to discover just how far they could go.

Lesson 1: Embracing Differences

Lesson 1:
Embracing Differences

Read: Uniquely You: Embracing the Power of Individuality

Strategy Middle/High School had a unique buzz in the air. The students were gathered in Mr. Unique's learning strategies class, excited about today's lesson. Mr. Unique was known for his inspiring and engaging teaching methods, and today, he had planned something special to help his students understand the importance of celebrating individuality and embracing differences.

The class included Na'ima, Naudia, Levi, and Nilan, each with unique strengths and challenges. As they settled into their seats, Mr. Unique began the lesson with a warm smile.

"Good morning, everyone! Today, we will talk about what makes each of us unique. We all have different strengths and challenges, and that's something to celebrate. Let's start by understanding how our differences make us stronger as individuals and as a community."

Mr. Unique handed out colorful sheets of paper and markers to each student. "I want you to draw or write about one thing that makes you unique. It can be a talent, a hobby, or something you love doing."

The classroom buzzed with activity as the students began to express their individuality.

Na'ima, who loved math, was the first to speak. "I drew a math book because I love solving math problems. But sometimes, I struggle with staying motivated to study regularly."

Next, Naudia shared her piece. "I wrote about my empathy for others. I care deeply about helping people and want to improve my conflict resolution skills."

Levi held up his drawing of a computer. "I drew this because I love technology and problem-solving. Sometimes, I find it hard to focus on one project at a time because there are so many interesting things to explore."

Nilan displayed his drawing of a soccer ball. "I love playing sports, especially soccer. My challenge is balancing my time between schoolwork and sports practice."

Mr. Unique looked at the colorful display of uniqueness before him and smiled. "Look at all these amazing strengths and interests! Each of you brings something special to our class. It's important to remember that we all learn and process information differently. That's what makes us unique."

He pointed to a poster on the wall that read, "Embrace Your Differences."

"Our differences are our strengths," he continued. "They make us who we are. This class will teach us to use our unique abilities to overcome challenges. We'll support each other and celebrate our progress together."

The students nodded, feeling a sense of pride and belonging. They understood that being different was something to be proud of and that their unique ways of learning were valuable.

To help reinforce this lesson, Mr. Unique organized an activity. He asked each student to pair up with someone they didn't usually work with and share their drawings. They discussed their strengths and challenges and brainstormed ways to support each other.

Na'ima and Nilan paired up. Na'ima offered to help Nilan with his math homework, suggesting they could study together after soccer practice. Nilan agreed and promised to share some time management tips that helped him balance school and sports.

Naudia and Levi paired up. Naudia suggested they create a weekly schedule to help Levi focus on his projects. Meanwhile, Levi offered to teach Naudia some problem-solving techniques he used in technology that could also be applied to resolving conflicts.

Mr. Unique watched his students engage in meaningful conversations, sharing ideas and supporting each other. He knew these interactions were vital in helping them understand the value of their differences and how they could work together to overcome their challenges.

As the class ended, Mr. Unique gathered the students in a circle. "Today, we've seen how our unique strengths and challenges can bring us closer together. By embracing our differences, we can learn from each other and grow stronger as individuals and as a community. Remember, it's okay to be different and to learn differently. That's what makes each of you special."

The students left the class with a renewed sense of confidence and understanding. They knew that their uniqueness was something to be celebrated and that together, they could achieve great things.

At Strategy Middle/High School, Mr. Unique's lesson on celebrating individuality and embracing differences had a lasting impact, creating a supportive and inclusive environment where every student felt valued and empowered to reach their full potential.

Lesson 2: Strengths and Interests

Lesson 2:
Strengths and Interests

Read: Power Up with Your Passions: Focusing on Strengths and Interests

Mrs. Grace's learning strategies class was exciting at Strategy Middle and High School. Today, Mrs. Grace planned a unique lesson to help her students understand the importance of focusing on their strengths and interests. The class included Noah, Kenlyn, Nia, and Lenny, each with unique talents and challenges.

Mrs. Grace began the lesson with a warm smile. "Good morning, everyone! Today, we're going to talk about our strengths and interests. Focusing on what we're good at and love doing is important because these strengths and interests can help us improve in challenging areas and make even the toughest classes more manageable."

She handed out colorful sheets of paper and markers to each student. "I want each of you to draw or write about one of your strengths and one of your interests. Think about how these can help you in other areas of your life and school."

The classroom buzzed with activity as the students began to express their strengths and interests.

Noah was the first to speak. He held up his drawing of a robot. "I love building things and inventing new gadgets. Sometimes, I struggle with staying organized, but focusing on my love for creating helps me find new ways to stay organized, like making a project schedule."

Next, Kenlyn shared her piece. "I drew a paintbrush because I love painting. It helps me express my feelings. When I have to write essays, which I find tough, I try to visualize my ideas as if I'm painting them. It makes writing more enjoyable."

Nia held up her drawing of a group of friends. "I love being around people and talking to them. Math is challenging sometimes, but I make it fun by forming study groups with my friends. We help each other out, and it doesn't feel like studying."

Lenny showed his work next. "I have a drawing of a science experiment. I love science, but I get overwhelmed by long reading assignments. I use my curiosity for science to break down the reading into smaller parts as I would with an experiment, which helps me understand better."

Mrs. Grace smiled and looked at the colorful display of strengths and interests. "Look at all these amazing talents and passions! Each of you brings something special to our class. Remembering that we all have challenging areas, but focusing on our strengths and interests can make those challenges more manageable."

She pointed to a poster on the wall that read, "Harness Your Strengths."

"Our strengths and interests are our superpowers," she continued. "They make us who we are. Even when we have to do tasks we're not always interested in, we can use our strengths and interests to get through those tough classes. For example, if you're great at building things like Noah, use that creativity to organize your notes. If you love socializing like Nia, form study groups for subjects you find hard."

The students nodded, feeling a sense of pride and motivation. They understood that by leveraging their strengths and interests, they could tackle their weaknesses and make less favorable subjects more enjoyable.

To reinforce this lesson, Mrs. Grace organized an activity. She asked each student to pair up and share their drawings. They discussed how they could use their strengths and interests to help each other with their challenges.

Noah and Kenlyn paired up. Noah shared his love for building and offered to help Kenlyn create visual aids for her essays. Kenlyn, in turn, offered to help Noah stay organized by painting a colorful schedule for his projects.

Nia and Lenny paired up. Nia suggested they form a study group for math, using her social skills to make it fun. Lenny offered to help Nia with science reading assignments by breaking them into smaller, manageable parts.

Mrs. Grace watched her students engage in meaningful conversations, sharing ideas and supporting each other. She knew that these interactions were vital in helping them understand the value of their strengths and interests and how they could use them to overcome their challenges.

As the class ended, Mrs. Grace gathered the students in a circle. "Today, we've seen how our unique strengths and interests can help us with our challenges. By focusing on what we love and what we're good at, we can make even the toughest tasks more manageable. Remember, everyone has to do things they don't always enjoy, but using your strengths can make those tasks easier and more enjoyable."

The students left the class with a renewed sense of confidence and understanding. They knew their strengths and interests were powerful tools that could help them tackle any challenge and make their learning journey more enjoyable and fulfilling.

At Strategy Middle and High School, Mrs. Grace's lesson on embracing strengths and interests had a lasting impact. It created a supportive and motivating environment where every student felt empowered to succeed.

Week 3: Self-Reflection and Goal Setting

Lesson 1: Reflecting on Personal Growth

Lesson 1:
Reflecting on Personal Growth

The Journey of Growth: Monitoring and Reflecting on Personal Progress

---

At Strategy Middle/High School, Ms. Progress's learning strategies class was well-known for focusing on personal growth and continuous improvement. The students in her class, including Kimiyah, Ahlani, Mason, and Nyrie, had been working hard to develop their strengths and overcome challenges. Today, Ms. Progress planned a lesson emphasizing the importance of monitoring and reflecting on their personal growth.

The classroom was filled with anticipation as Ms. Progress began the lesson with a welcoming smile. "Good morning, everyone! Today, we will discuss the importance of monitoring your progress and reflecting on your personal growth. This is crucial because it helps us understand how far we've come and what we must do to keep improving."

Ms. Progress handed out reflective journals to each student. "I want each of you to think about your journey so far. Write down one goal you set for yourself at the beginning of the year, the steps you took to achieve it, and your progress. Then, think about what you can do to continue growing."

The students eagerly opened their journals and began writing. After a few minutes, Ms. Progress asked them to share their reflections.

Kimiyah was the first to speak. "At the beginning of the year, I set a goal to improve my executive functioning skills. I started using a planner to organize my assignments and set reminders for important tasks. I've become much better at managing my time, but I can still improve by setting more specific daily goals."

Ahlani shared her reflection next. "My goal was to stay more organized, especially with my history notes. I created a color-coded system for my notes and started reviewing them regularly. It's helped me a lot, but I must stay consistent, especially when busy with other subjects."

Mason, who had a passion for music, spoke about his journey. "I wanted to manage my performance anxiety better. I started practicing mindfulness and meditation before my performances, which has helped. Now, I want to focus on performing more confidently in front of larger audiences."

Nyrie, an avid reader, shared his progress. "I aimed to improve my reading comprehension. I began using graphic organizers to track the main ideas and details in the texts I read. This has helped me understand and remember what I read much better. My next step is to apply these strategies to more complex texts."

Ms. Progress smiled as she listened to her students. "I'm so proud of all of you. Monitoring and reflecting on your progress is essential because it helps you see what works and what doesn't. It also motivates you to keep pushing forward."

She then introduced an activity to reinforce the lesson. "Now, let's pair up and discuss our reflections. Share your goals, your progress, and your plans for continuing growth. Give each other feedback and suggestions."

Kimiyah paired up with Ahlani. They shared their reflections and gave each other helpful tips. Kimiyah suggested that Ahlani use a checklist to stay consistent with her note review, while Ahlani recommended that Kimiyah break down her daily goals into smaller, more manageable tasks.

Mason and Nyrie formed another pair. Mason suggested that Nyrie try reading aloud to improve comprehension of complex texts, while Nyrie encouraged Mason to record his performances and watch them build confidence.

Ms. Progress watched her students engage in meaningful conversations, sharing ideas and supporting each other's growth. She knew these interactions were vital in helping them understand the importance of continuous reflection and monitoring.

As the class ended, Ms. Progress gathered the students in a circle. "Today, we've learned that monitoring our progress and reflecting on our growth helps us understand our strengths and areas for improvement. It's a journey that requires patience and perseverance. Remember, it's okay to celebrate your achievements and recognize where you need to grow. By doing so, you'll continue to evolve and reach your full potential."

The students left the class with a renewed sense of purpose and motivation. They understood that personal growth was an ongoing journey, and by monitoring and reflecting on their progress, they could continue to improve and succeed.

At Strategy Middle/High School, Ms. Progress's lesson on the importance of monitoring and reflecting on personal growth had a lasting impact. It created a supportive and motivating environment where students felt empowered to achieve their goals and reach new heights.

Lesson 2:
Setting Personal Goals

Read: Goals for Greatness: Empowering Success in Academics and Life

At Strategy Middle/High School, Mr. Goals's learning strategies class was always filled with energy and enthusiasm. Today, Mr. Goals had planned an essential lesson about setting personal goals, which he believed was crucial for improving academics and personal life. The students in his class included Ahlani, Nyrie, Kenlyn, Nia, and Lenny, each eager to learn how they could better their lives by setting clear and attainable goals.

Mr. Goals started the class with his usual warm smile. "Good morning, everyone! Today, we're going to talk about setting personal goals. Setting goals is important because it gives us direction and purpose. It helps us focus on what we want and how to get there."

He handed out goal-setting worksheets to each student. "I want you all to think about one academic and personal goal you want to achieve. Write down the goal, why it's important to you, and the steps you will take to reach it."

The classroom buzzed with activity as the students began to write down their goals.

Ahlani was the first to share. "For my academic goal, I want to improve my organization for history class. I always end up losing my notes. I will use a color-coded system and review my notes every week. I aim to read one book monthly because I love reading but never find the time."

Nyrie followed with his goals: " For my academic goal, I want to improve my reading comprehension. I'll start using graphic organizers to track the main ideas and details. For my personal goal, I want to join the school's debate team to improve my public speaking skills."

Kenlyn shared her goals next. "My academic goal is to improve my writing skills, especially essays. I'll practice writing a little daily and ask for teacher feedback. My goal is to finish an art project I've been working on. I'll set aside time each weekend to work on it."

Nia was excited to share her goals. "For my academic goal, I want to improve my math grades. I'll form a study group with my friends and practice problems every day. I aim to spend more time with my family, so I'll plan a fun family activity every weekend."

Lenny shared his goals last. "I want to get better at science experiments. I'll start by reading the instructions more carefully and asking for help when needed. My personal goal is to learn how to play the guitar. I'll practice for 30 minutes every day."

Mr. Goals listened attentively to each student, proud of the thought they had put into their goals. "These are fantastic goals! Setting personal goals helps you focus on your goals and keeps you motivated. It's important to break down your goals into smaller, manageable steps and to monitor your progress regularly."

To reinforce this lesson, Mr. Goals organized an activity. He asked each student to pair up and discuss their goals with a partner. They shared their steps and provided each other with suggestions and encouragement.

Ahlani paired up with Kenlyn. Ahlani suggested that Kenlyn create a checklist for her writing practice, while Kenlyn encouraged Ahlani to set specific reading times during the week to reach her book-a-month goal.

Nyrie and Nia formed another pair. Nyrie suggested that Nia use flashcards for her math practice, while Nia encouraged Nyrie to start a public speaking club to practice his debate skills more frequently.

Lenny and Mr. Goals paired up as well. Mr. Goals suggested that Lenny record his guitar playing to track his progress. At the same time, Lenny shared his excitement about improving his science experiments and promised to help Mr. Goals with any classroom demonstrations.

As the class ended, Mr. Goals gathered the students in a circle. "Today, we've learned that personal goals are essential for our growth. Goals help us stay focused, motivated, and on track. Remember, achieving your goals takes time and effort, but you can reach them with determination and the right steps."

The students left the class with a renewed sense of purpose and excitement. They understood that setting clear and attainable goals could significantly improve their academic performance and personal lives. They were ready to take on their goals with the support of their teacher and classmates.

At Strategy Middle/High School, Mr. Goals's lesson on setting personal goals had a lasting impact. It created a supportive and motivating environment where every student felt empowered to strive for their best and achieve their dreams.

Week 4: Unleashing My Powers

Lesson 1:
Introduction to Meditation, Executive Functioning, and Good Habits

Lesson 1: Introduction to Meditation, Executive Functioning, and Good Habits

Read: Unleashing My Powers

At Strategy Middle/High School, Mrs. Grace's learning strategies class was abuzz with curiosity. Today, she had a special lesson planned called "Unleashing My Powers." Mrs. Grace wanted to introduce her students to three powerful tools to help them succeed in school, at home, and in their personal lives: meditation, executive functioning skills, and good habits. The students, Noah, Na'ima, Naudia, Levi, Nilan, and Mason, were eager to learn how these new skills could make a difference in their lives.

Mrs. Grace began the lesson with a warm smile. "Good morning, everyone! Today, we're going to discover our inner superpowers. By learning meditation, executive functioning skills, and good habits, you can unleash your full potential and achieve great things in school and your personal lives."

She handed out colorful worksheets outlining meditation basics, executive functioning, and good habits. "Let's start with meditation. Meditation is a powerful tool that helps calm your mind and improve your focus. It can reduce stress and help you feel more centered."

Noah, who often struggled with staying focused on his schoolwork, was intrigued. "How do we meditate, Mrs. Grace?"

"Let's do a simple exercise," Mrs. Grace said. "Close your eyes, sit comfortably, and take a deep breath. Hold it for a moment, then slowly breathe out. Focus on your breath, and let go of any distracting thoughts."

The students followed her instructions, and the room fell silent as they practiced breathing deeply and focusing on their breath. After a few minutes, Mrs. Grace asked them to open their eyes.

"How do you feel?" she asked.

"I feel more relaxed," Na'ima said. This could help me when I am stressed about my math homework."

Mrs. Grace nodded. "Exactly, Na'ima. Meditation can help you stay calm and focused, essential for managing stress and staying on task."

Next, Mrs. Grace introduced executive functioning skills. "Executive functioning skills include planning, organization, time management, and problem-solving. These skills help you stay organized and make smart decisions."

Naudia, who often felt overwhelmed by her school assignments, was curious. "How can we improve our executive functioning skills?"

"Start by using a planner," Mrs. Grace suggested. "Write down your assignments, due dates, and other important tasks. Break big projects into smaller, manageable steps. This will help you stay organized and reduce stress."

Levi, who loved technology, used a digital planner to keep track of his assignments. "I think using a planner will help me stay on top of my work and not forget important deadlines," he said.

"That's a great idea, Levi," Mrs. Grace said. "Finding a system that works for you is key to improving your executive functioning skills."

Finally, Mrs. Grace talked about good habits. "Good habits are behaviors you practice regularly that positively impact your life. They can help you be more productive, healthy, and happy."

Nilan, who loved sports, realized he could develop good habits to improve his athletic performance. "What are some examples of good habits, Mrs. Grace?"

"Good habits can include setting a regular bedtime to ensure you get enough sleep, eating healthy foods, and setting aside time each day for exercise or study," Mrs. Grace explained. "These habits help you build a routine that supports your goals."

Mason, who often felt anxious before his music performances, saw how good habits could help him manage his anxiety. "If I practice meditation and set aside time each day to practice my music, I think I'll feel more confident and less anxious."

Mrs. Grace smiled. "Exactly, Mason. You can unleash your full potential and achieve success in all areas by integrating meditation, executive functioning skills, and good habits into your daily life."

To reinforce the lesson, Mrs. Grace asked each student to think about how they could use these powers in their own lives. They wrote down their thoughts and shared them with the class.

Noah said, "I'll use meditation to improve my focus during study sessions and use a planner to keep track of my assignments."

Na'ima shared, "I'll practice meditation to manage my stress and develop the habit of reviewing my math notes daily."

Naudia added, "I'll use a planner to organize my schoolwork and set a regular study schedule."

Levi said, "I'll use a digital planner to stay organized and set aside time each day for coding practice."

Nilan said, "I'll develop good habits like eating healthy and getting enough sleep to improve my sports performance."

Mason concluded, "I'll practice meditation to manage my anxiety and set a regular practice schedule for my music."

Mrs. Grace was proud of her students. "By using these powers, you can achieve great things in school and your personal life. Remember, it's about making small changes and practicing these skills regularly."

The students left the class feeling empowered and ready to unleash their full potential. They understood that by integrating meditation, executive functioning skills, and good habits into their daily lives, they could overcome challenges and achieve their goals.

At Strategy Middle/High School, Mrs. Grace's "Unleashing My Powers" lesson had a lasting impact. It created a supportive and motivating environment where every student felt empowered to succeed academically and personally.

Lesson 2: Personal Action Plan

Lesson 2:
Personal Action Plan

Mapping Your Success: Creating a Personal Action Plan

At Strategy Middle/High School, Mr. Plan's learning strategies class was known for its practical approach to achieving goals. Today, Mr. Plan had a special lesson on planning and writing a Personal Action Plan. The students, Ahlani, Nia, Lenny, Kenlyn, and Nyrie, were eager to learn how to create a structured plan to achieve their personal and academic goals.

Mr. Plan began the class with a smile. "Good morning, everyone! Today, we will learn how to create a Personal Action Plan. This plan will help you identify your goals, the steps needed to achieve them, and how to monitor your progress. By having a clear plan, you can stay focused and motivated."

He handed out worksheets outlining the steps for creating a Personal Action Plan: "Let's start by thinking about one academic goal and one personal goal you want to achieve."

The students eagerly started writing down their goals.

Ahlani was the first to share. "My academic goal is to improve my grades in history. I find it hard to keep track of all the events and dates. I aim to read more books because I love reading but never find the time."

Mr. Plan nodded. "Great goals, Ahlani! Now, let's break them down into actionable steps. What can you do to improve your history grades?"

Ahlani thought for a moment. "I can start by reviewing my notes daily, making flashcards for important dates, and asking for help when I don't understand something."

"Excellent," Mr. Plan said. "And for your personal goal?"

"I can set aside 30 minutes daily for reading," Ahlani replied.

Nia shared her goals next. "My academic goal is to get better at math. I struggle with understanding some concepts. My personal goal is to spend more quality time with my family."

Mr. Plan asked, "What steps will you take to improve math?"

Nia answered, "I'll join a study group, practice math problems daily, and ask my teacher for extra help."

"And for your personal goal?" Mr. Plan asked.

"I can plan a family activity every weekend," Nia said.

Lenny was up next. "I want to improve my science grades. I get overwhelmed by the experiments. My personal goal is to learn to play the guitar."

Mr. Plan encouraged him to break down his goals. "What steps can you take for your science goal?"

Lenny replied, "I can read the experiment instructions carefully, ask my teacher for clarification, and practice the experiments at home if possible."

"And for learning the guitar?" Mr. Plan asked.

"I can practice for 30 minutes daily and take lessons once a week," Lenny said.

Kenlyn shared her goals. "I want to improve my writing skills, especially essays. My personal goal is to complete an art project I've been working on."

Mr. Plan asked, "What steps will you take to achieve your writing goal?"

Kenlyn replied, "I'll write daily, read more to improve my vocabulary, and ask for teacher feedback."

"And for your art project?" Mr. Plan asked.

"I can set aside time each weekend to work on it," Kenlyn said.

Finally, Nyrie shared his goals. "I want to get better at public speaking. I get nervous. My personal goal is to join the school's debate team."

Mr. Plan asked, "What steps can you take to improve your public speaking?"

Nyrie answered, "I can practice speaking in front of a mirror, join a public speaking club, and volunteer to speak in class more often."

"And for joining the debate team?" Mr. Plan asked.

"I can attend the meetings and participate in the practice debates," Nyrie said.

Mr. Plan smiled at his students. "These are all fantastic goals and actionable steps. Now, let's put them into your Personal Action Plans. Write down your goals, your steps, and how you'll monitor your progress."

The students worked diligently on their plans, and Mr. Plan moved around the room, offering guidance and support. Once they were finished, he asked them to share their plans with a partner and discuss how they would hold each other accountable.

Ahlani paired up with Nia. They shared their plans and promised to check in with each other every week to discuss their progress. Lenny and Kenlyn did the same, as did Nyrie and Mr. Plan, who had also written his own goals to share with the class.

As the class ended, Mr. Plan gathered everyone in a circle. "Today, we've learned the importance of planning and writing a Personal Action Plan. You can achieve great things by breaking your goals into actionable steps and monitoring your progress. Remember to support each other and stay focused on your goals."

The students left the class feeling empowered and motivated, ready to implement their Personal Action Plans. They understood that with a clear plan and the support of their classmates and teachers, they could achieve their goals and succeed academically and personally.

At Strategy Middle/High School, Mr. Plan's lesson on creating a Personal Action Plan had a lasting impact, helping students develop the skills needed to achieve their dreams and reach their full potential.

Unit 2:

The Superpower of Meditation
(Weeks 5-9)

Introduction to Unit 2: The Superpower of Meditation

Welcome, Strategy Middle/High School students, to Unit 2 of our Learning Strategies class: The Superpower of Meditation. Over the next five weeks, we will embark on an exciting journey to discover the incredible benefits of meditation and how it can transform our lives. Our journey is divided into five key sections:

Week 5: The Basics of Meditation

This week, we will lay the foundation by learning what meditation is and why it is important. You will explore simple techniques like deep breathing and mindfulness to help calm your mind and body. These basic practices will be the stepping stones to mastering the art of meditation.

Week 6: Building Meditation Practice

As we move into the second week, we will focus on building a consistent meditation practice. You will learn how to create a quiet space, set a regular meditation schedule, and practice different meditation methods. Consistency is critical to reaping the full benefits of meditation.

Week 7: Applying Meditation to Daily Life

In Week 3, we will practice meditation beyond the classroom and into our daily lives. You will learn to use meditation techniques to manage stress, stay focused, and maintain calm throughout your day. We will explore practical applications, including how to meditate during stressful situations like exams or public speaking.

Week 8: Advanced Meditation Techniques

By Week 4, you will be ready to dive into more advanced meditation techniques. We will explore guided imagery, body scanning, and mantra meditation. These techniques will deepen your practice and enhance your ability to relax and focus.

Week 9: Integrating Meditation with Learning

In our final week, we will integrate meditation with your learning process. You will learn how meditation can improve your concentration, memory, and overall academic performance. We will also discuss how meditation can help you build better habits and enhance your executive functioning skills, such as planning, organizing, and problem-solving.

How Meditation Helps Students with Disabilities

Meditation is a powerful tool that can significantly benefit students with disabilities. It helps in various areas where you may lack proficiency due to your individual challenges:

- **Overcoming Test Anxiety:** Meditation techniques like deep breathing and visualization can reduce anxiety during tests, allowing you to approach exams with a calm and focused mind.
- **Reducing Fear of Public Speaking:** Visualization and positive affirmations can build your confidence, making speaking in front of others easier.
- **Managing Anger and Emotions:** Techniques like body scanning and mantra repetition help control anger and other intense emotions, promoting emotional stability.
- **Improving Executive Functioning Skills:** Meditation enhances focus, memory, and organizational skills, which are crucial for effective learning and daily life management.
- **Building New Habits:** Consistent meditation helps form new, positive habits supporting overall well-being and success.

As we journey through this unit, remember that meditation is a personal practice. Each of you will find what works best for you. By embracing the superpower of meditation, you will unlock new potentials within yourself, helping you succeed in school and all areas of your life.

Let's embark on this transformative journey together and discover the incredible benefits of meditation!

Week 5: The Basics of Meditation

Lesson 1: What is Meditation?

Lesson 1:
What is Meditation?

Conduct Pre Survey

Read: Title: Discovering the Basics of Meditation: A Transformative Journey

In the heart of Goodness, the Strategy Middle/High School students were about to embark on a transformative journey. Led by their compassionate teacher, Ms. Calmness, the class, known as Learning Strategies, was a haven where students could explore new ways to overcome their challenges and unlock their true potential.

Discovering the Basics of Meditation

Ms. Calmness stood before her students, her voice soothing and kind. "Today, we begin our adventure into the world of meditation," she said. "Meditation is a powerful tool that can help you manage stress, focus better, and feel more at peace."

Noah, who often felt overwhelmed by test anxiety, listened intently. His hands would shake, and his mind would race during exams, making concentrating hard. Kenlyn, who loved stories but dreaded speaking in front of others, leaned forward with curiosity. Her fear of public speaking often made her miss out on sharing her beautiful ideas. Nia, who sometimes struggled with her learning disability, looked hopeful. She usually felt overwhelmed by schoolwork and needed a way to calm her mind. Lenny was fiery, and Ahlani, who wanted to help her family and community, was eager to learn. Lenny's anger would flare up quickly, causing problems with friends, while Ahlani wished to bring peace and focus to her loved ones.

"Let's start with a simple breathing exercise," Ms. Calmness suggested. "Close your eyes, sit comfortably, and take a deep breath for four counts. Hold it for four, and then breathe out for four."

The students followed her instructions, feeling their bodies relax with each breath. Ms. Calmness continued, "This is called mindful breathing. It helps calm your mind and body, making it easier to focus and feel at ease."

Noah's Journey with Mindful Breathing

Noah practiced mindful breathing daily. As he took deep breaths, he imagined a peaceful beach, the sound of waves calming his mind. When test day arrived, Noah used his breathing technique. His anxiety began to melt away, and he could focus on the questions with a clear mind. The simple mindful breathing helped Noah feel more confident and less anxious during exams.

Kenlyn's Discovery of Positive Visualization

Kenlyn was introduced to a meditation technique called positive visualization. "Close your eyes and picture yourself speaking confidently in front of the class," Ms. Calmness instructed. Kenlyn imagined herself standing tall, her voice clear and strong, her classmates listening intently.

By practicing this visualization, Kenlyn began to feel less fearful. She realized she could overcome her fear of public speaking by calming her mind and visualizing success. This newfound confidence encouraged her to share her stories and ideas more freely.

Nia's Embrace of Mantra Repetition

For Nia, Ms. Calmness introduced the technique of mantra repetition. "Choose a calming word or phrase, like 'peace' or 'I am calm,'" she suggested. Nia chose the word "strong." Whenever she felt overwhelmed by her schoolwork, she would close her eyes and repeat "strong" silently.

This simple practice helped Nia feel more in control and less stressed. By focusing on her mantra, she found a way to calm her mind and approach her tasks more confidently.

Lenny's Use of Body Scanning

Lenny, who struggled with anger, was introduced to body scanning. Ms. Calmness guided the class, "Sit quietly and focus on each part of your body, from your toes to the top of your head. Relax each part as you go along."

Lenny practiced this every morning. When he felt anger rising, he would close his eyes and do a quick body scan. The anger began to fade, replaced by a sense of peace. This technique helped Lenny control his emotions and interact more positively with his friends.

Ahlani's Creation of a Meditation Corner

Ahlani saw the power of meditation for herself, her family, and her community. She shared the mindful breathing technique with her younger brother and taught the body scan to her friends. Together, they created a peaceful corner at home where anyone could meditate.

Through these practices, Ahlani brought a sense of calm and focus to her home. She realized that meditation could be a powerful tool for improving the well-being of those around her.

Conclusion

As they discovered the basics of meditation, Noah, Kenlyn, Nia, Lenny, and Ahlani found simple yet powerful tools to help them manage their challenges. Through mindful breathing, positive visualization, mantra repetition, and body scanning, they learned to calm their minds and bodies, paving the way for tremendous success at school, home, and community.

With Ms. Calmness's guidance, they embraced meditation as a lifelong superpower. This journey into the basics of meditation marked the beginning of a transformative adventure, showing them that with practice and dedication, they could overcome any obstacle and unlock their true potential.

Lesson 2: Simple Meditation Techniques

Breath
Don't try to "calm your mind." If your mind starts wandering, recognize it and return to appreciating the sensations of your breath.

Emotions
Long-term meditators show increased size in brain regions associated with emotional regulation, which may help cultivate positive emotions.

Eyes
If you want the experience to be more body-based, close your eyes. If you want to feel more anchored in your space, keep them open.

Arms
Relax your shoulders and arms, letting your hands rest on your thighs. Place one hand on another in your lap.

Legs
If you're sitting in a chair, keep your feet flat on the floor and your spine straight. If you're sitting cross-legged on a cushion, have your knees below your hips.

Time
Meditation isn't about length; it's about frequency. You don't get strong by lifting weights once. Meditating for about 5 to 10 minutes every day is a great start.

Lesson 2: Simple Meditation Techniques

The Power of Simple Meditation Techniques

In the bustling town of Goodness, Strategy Middle/High School was known for its dedication to helping students achieve their full potential. Among the many classes offered, the Learning Strategies class, led by the ever-calm Mr. Stressfree, was a sanctuary for students seeking new ways to overcome their challenges.

The Beginning of the Journey

Na'ima, Naudia, Nyrie, and Mason were students in Mr. Stressfree's class. Each of them had their unique struggles. Na'ima often felt anxious during tests, Naudia was overwhelmed by her learning disability, Nyrie had trouble focusing, and Mason struggled with managing his emotions.

One sunny morning, Mr. Stressfree greeted his students with a warm smile. "Today, we're going to explore the power of simple meditation techniques," he announced. "These practices can help you manage stress, improve your focus, and enhance your overall well-being."

Discovering Mindful Breathing

"Let's start with mindful breathing," Mr. Stressfree said. "It's a simple technique to help calm your mind and body."

He guided the students to sit comfortably, close their eyes, and take deep breaths. "Breathe in for four counts, hold it for four, and breathe out for four."

Na'ima felt the immediate effects. The racing thoughts that usually accompanied her test anxiety began to slow down. She imagined herself in a peaceful garden, with each breath bringing her closer to calm.

Embracing Positive Visualization

Next, Mr. Stressfree introduced positive visualization. "This technique helps you envision success and reduce fear," he explained. "Close your eyes and picture yourself succeeding in a challenging task."

Naudia closed her eyes and visualized herself quickly understanding and completing her schoolwork. She imagined the satisfaction of mastering complex concepts, which gave her a newfound sense of confidence.

The Power of Mantra Repetition

Mr. Stressfree then introduced mantra repetition. "Choose a calming word or phrase, like 'peace' or 'I am strong,' and repeat it silently."

Nyrie chose the phrase "I am focused." As he repeated it, he felt his wandering thoughts settle. This simple practice helped him concentrate better in and out of the classroom.

Practicing Body Scanning

"Now, let's try body scanning," Mr. Stressfree suggested. "Focus on each part of your body, from your toes to your head, and relax each part as you go along."

Mason found this technique particularly helpful. By concentrating on relaxing his body, he felt a significant reduction in his usual tension and stress. The body scan allowed him to manage his emotions more effectively.

Applying Meditation to Daily Life

As the weeks passed, Mr. Stressfree encouraged his students to integrate these meditation techniques into their daily lives. "Meditation is not just a classroom activity," he said. "It's a tool you can use anytime you feel stressed, anxious, or unfocused."

Na'ima began using mindful breathing before every test, which helped her stay calm and focused. Naudia practiced positive visualization before tackling challenging assignments, boosting her confidence. Nyrie repeated his mantra whenever his concentration slipped, keeping his mind sharp. Mason used body scanning to calm himself whenever he felt his emotions getting the better of him.

Conclusion

The students of Strategy Middle/High School found that these simple meditation techniques made a world of difference in their lives. Under Mr. Stressfree's gentle guidance, they discovered that meditation was a powerful tool for overcoming their unique challenges.

Na'ima, Naudia, Nyrie, and Mason felt more in control of their minds and bodies. They realized that with regular practice, meditation could help them succeed academically and improve their overall well-being.

With their new superpower of meditation, the students were ready to face any challenge, proving that even the most straightforward techniques could lead to profound transformations.

Week 6: Building a Meditation Practice

Lesson 1: Establishing a Routine

Lesson 1:
Establishing a Routine

Building a Meditation Practice: A Path to Academic Success

In the heart of Goodness, Strategy Middle/High School was renowned for its innovative approach to learning. Among the school's dedicated faculty was Mr. Stressfree, the beloved Learning Strategies teacher, who had a special gift for helping students manage stress and excel academically.

Kimiyah, Levi, and Nilan were three students in Mr. Stressfree's class, each with unique challenges. Kimiyah often felt overwhelmed by the sheer volume of her schoolwork. Levi struggled with focusing in class, and Nilan needed help managing his time effectively. They all admired Mr. Stressfree for his calm demeanor and wise advice.

The Importance of Building a Meditation Practice

One crisp Monday morning, Mr. Stressfree gathered his students for a particular lesson. "Today, we're going to talk about building a meditation practice and establishing a routine," he began, his voice as soothing as ever. "Meditation is not just a tool for relaxation; it can also help you succeed academically."

Kimiyah raised her hand. "How can meditation help us with schoolwork, Mr. Stressfree?"

Mr. Stressfree smiled. "Great question, Kimiyah. Building a consistent meditation practice helps improve your focus, reduces stress, and enhances your ability to manage time. These skills are crucial for academic success."

Establishing a Routine

Levi looked intrigued. "So, how do we start building this practice?"

"First, we need to establish a routine," Mr. Stressfree explained. "Set aside a specific time each day for meditation. It could be in the morning before school, during a break, or in the evening before bed. Consistency is key."

Kimiyah's Morning Routine

Kimiyah decided to try meditating every morning before school. She set her alarm ten minutes earlier and found a quiet spot in her room. She started with mindful breathing, focusing on her breath and clearing her mind. At first, it was challenging, but as days passed, she noticed that she felt calmer and more prepared for the day ahead.

Levi's Break Time Meditation

Levi chose to meditate during his lunch break. He found a quiet corner in the school library and practiced positive visualization. He would close his eyes and picture himself completing his assignments and understanding complex concepts. This practice helped him feel more confident and focused in class.

Nilan's Evening Reflection

Nilan decided to meditate in the evening. After finishing his homework, he would sit quietly and practice body scanning. He focused on relaxing each part of his body, letting go of the day's tension. This routine helped him unwind and improved his sleep, making him more alert and ready for the next day.

The Transformation

Weeks passed, and the students began to notice significant changes. Kimiyah felt less overwhelmed and more organized. Levi's focus in class improved, and he found it easier to concentrate on his studies. Nilan's time management skills were enhanced, and he no longer felt rushed or stressed.

One day, Mr. Stressfree asked the class, "How has building a meditation practice and establishing a routine helped you?"

Kimiyah was the first to speak. "Meditating every morning has made a huge difference. I feel more in control and ready to tackle my schoolwork."

Levi nodded. "I agree. Visualizing my success during lunch helps me stay focused and confident throughout the day."

Nilan added, "Evening meditation has improved my sleep and time management. I feel more balanced and less stressed."

Conclusion

Mr. Stressfree beamed with pride. "I'm glad to hear that meditation is helping you. Building a practice takes time and dedication, but the benefits are worth it. By establishing a routine, you are setting yourselves up for success in school and life."

And so, Kimiyah, Levi, and Nilan continued their meditation practices, finding new strengths and abilities within themselves. With Mr. Stressfree's guidance, they learned that consistency, focus, and a calm mind were the keys to unlocking their academic potential. In the tranquil town of Goodness, the Strategy Middle/High School students discovered that the path to success was paved with mindfulness and meditation.

Lesson 2:
Using Meditation for Stress Relief

Using Meditation for Stress Relief: A Journey to Academic and Personal Growth

In the vibrant town of Goodness, Strategy Middle/High School was known for its innovative and nurturing environment. Among the many dedicated teachers, Ms. Relief stood out for her deep understanding of the students' challenges. She taught the Learning Strategies class, where students learned how to manage stress and improve their academic performance.

The Danger of Stress

One bright morning, Ms. Relief gathered her students for an important lesson. Noah, Kenlyn, Mason, Ahlani, Nia, Lenny, Naudia, Na'ima, Nyrie, Kimiyah, Levi, and Nilan were all present, each facing their unique struggles. Ms. Relief began with a severe tone.

"Today, we're going to talk about stress and its impact on our lives," she said. "Stress can affect academic performance, personal growth, and overall well-being. When we are stressed, it's harder to concentrate, remember things, and even stay motivated."

The students listened intently as Ms. Relief continued. "Chronic stress can lead to anxiety, depression, and physical health problems. It's essential to find ways to manage stress effectively. One powerful tool we can use is meditation."

Noah and Kenlyn's Stress Relief through Mindful Breathing

Ms. Relief turned to Noah and Kenlyn. "Noah, Kenlyn, let's start with mindful breathing. This technique can help calm your mind and reduce anxiety."

She guided them to sit comfortably, close their eyes, and take deep breaths. "Breathe in for four counts, hold it for four, and breathe out for four."

Noah, who often felt overwhelmed by test anxiety, and Kenlyn, who dreaded public speaking, found immediate relief. As they practiced mindful breathing, they felt their stress melting away, replaced by a sense of calm and focus.

Mason and Ahlani's Positive Visualization

Next, Ms. Relief introduced positive visualization to Mason and Ahlani. "Close your eyes and imagine yourself succeeding in a stressful situation. "Picture yourself feeling calm and confident."

Mason, who struggled with managing his emotions, visualized himself handling conflicts peacefully. Ahlani, who wanted to bring peace to her family and community, imagined herself spreading calmness through her actions. This technique helped them build confidence and reduce stress.

Nia and Lenny's Mantra Repetition

"Nia, Lenny, let's try mantra repetition," Ms. Relief suggested. "Choose a calming word or phrase, like 'peace' or 'I am strong,' and repeat it silently."

Nia, who often felt overwhelmed by her learning disability, chose the mantra "I am capable." Lenny, who struggled with anger, decided, "I am calm." They found a way to center themselves and reduce stress by repeating their mantras.

Naudia and Na'ima's Body Scanning

"Naudia, Na'ima, we'll practice body scanning," Ms. Relief continued. "Focus on each part of your body, from your toes to your head, and relax each part as you go along."

Naudia, who often felt overwhelmed by schoolwork, and Na'ima, who dealt with anxiety, felt the tension leaving their bodies as they practiced this technique. Body scanning helped them relax and manage their stress more effectively.

Nyrie, Kimiyah, Levi, and Nilan's Routine Building

Finally, Ms. Relief addressed Nyrie, Kimiyah, Levi, and Nilan. "Building a meditation routine can help you manage stress consistently. Find a time each day to practice these techniques."

Nyrie decided to meditate every morning, Kimiyah during her lunch break, Levi before starting his homework, and Nilan before bed. Incorporating meditation into their daily routines made it easier to handle stress and stay focused on their goals.

The Transformation

As the weeks passed, the students noticed significant changes in their lives. Noah felt more confident during tests, Kenlyn spoke more freely in class, Mason managed his emotions better, and Ahlani spread calmness at home. Nia and Lenny found new ways to handle their stress, Naudia and Na'ima felt more relaxed, and Nyrie, Kimiyah, Levi, and Nilan saw improvements in their academic performance and personal growth.

Conclusion

Ms. Relief beamed with pride as she observed the positive changes in her students. "Remember, stress is a part of life, but it doesn't have to control you. By using meditation techniques, you can manage stress effectively and unlock your full potential."

The students of Strategy Middle/High School realized that meditation was not just a tool for relaxation but a powerful practice for achieving academic success and personal growth. With Ms. Relief's guidance, they learned to navigate life's challenges with calmness and confidence, proving that the journey to overcoming stress was a path to greatness.

Week 7: Applying Meditation to Daily Life

Lesson 1: Meditation for Focus and Concentration

Lesson 1:
Meditation for Focus and Concentration

Applying Meditation to Daily Life: A Path to Focus and Academic Success

At Strategy Middle/High School, students constantly sought new ways to improve their academic performance and personal growth. Among the school's dedicated faculty was Mr. Focus, a Learning Strategies teacher known for his innovative approaches to helping students achieve their best.

The Challenge

Kimiyah, Levi, and Nilan were three students in Mr. Focus's class. Each faced unique challenges with focus and concentration. Kimiyah struggled to stay organized and often felt overwhelmed by her assignments. Levi had trouble concentrating during long study sessions, and Nilan struggled to manage his time effectively.

One sunny afternoon, Mr. Focus gathered his students for an important lesson. "Today, we're going to learn about the power of meditation and how applying it to our daily lives can improve focus and concentration," he announced. "Meditation isn't just for relaxation; it's a tool to help you succeed academically."

The Introduction to Meditation for Focus

Mr. Focus began by explaining the basics of meditation. "Meditation helps train your mind to stay present and focused. By practicing regularly, you can improve your ability to concentrate on tasks and manage distractions."

Kimiyah raised her hand. "How can meditation help me with my assignments, Mr. Focus?"

"Great question, Kimiyah," Mr. Focus replied. "Let's explore some specific techniques that can help."

Mindful Breathing for Kimiyah

Mr. Focus guided the class through a simple mindful breathing exercise. "Sit comfortably, close your eyes, and focus on your breath. Take a deep breath in for four counts, hold it for four, and breathe out for four."

Kimiyah followed along, feeling her mind clear with each breath. "When you feel overwhelmed by assignments, take a few minutes to practice mindful breathing," Mr. Focus suggested. "It will help calm your mind and improve your ability to focus."

Positive Visualization for Levi

Next, Mr. Focus introduced positive visualization. "Close your eyes and imagine yourself completing a study session or understanding a complex topic," he instructed.

Levi closed his eyes and visualized himself studying efficiently, staying focused, and feeling confident. "By visualizing success, you train your mind to focus on positive outcomes," Mr. Focus explained. "This can boost your concentration and motivation."

Mantra Repetition for Nilan

Mr. Focus then taught the class about mantra repetition. "Choose a calming word or phrase, like 'focus' or 'I am capable,' and repeat it silently while you study."

Nilan chose the mantra "I am focused." He felt his mind become more centered and attentive as he repeated it. "Using a mantra can help anchor your mind and reduce distractions," Mr. Focus said. It's a powerful way to enhance concentration."

Integrating Meditation into Daily Life

Mr. Focus emphasized the importance of integrating meditation into daily routines. "Consistency is key," he said. "Set aside a specific time each day to practice these techniques. Regular practice will strengthen your ability to focus, Whether in the morning, during a break, or before bed."

The Transformation

As the weeks passed, Kimiyah, Levi, and Nilan diligently practiced meditation techniques. Kimiyah used mindful breathing to manage her assignments, Levi visualized success before study sessions, and Nilan repeated his mantra to stay focused.

They soon noticed significant improvements. Kimiyah felt more organized and less overwhelmed, Levi's concentration improved during study sessions, and Nilan became more efficient with time management. Their grades reflected these positive changes, and they felt more confident in their academic abilities.

Conclusion

One day, Mr. Focus asked his students to reflect on their experiences. "How has applying meditation to your daily life helped you?"

Kimiyah smiled. "Mindful breathing helps me stay calm and focused on my assignments. I don't feel as overwhelmed anymore."

Levi nodded. "Positive visualization boosts my confidence and concentration during study sessions. I feel more motivated."

Nilan added, "Repeating my mantra keeps me centered and focused. I'm better at managing my time and staying on task."

Mr. Focus beamed with pride. "I'm glad to hear that meditation is helping you. Remember, the key to success is consistency. Keep practicing, and you'll continue to see improvements."

The students of Strategy Middle/High School realized that meditation was not just a tool for relaxation but a powerful practice for achieving academic success. With Mr. Focus's guidance, they learned to apply meditation to their daily lives, unlocking their full potential and paving the way for a bright future.

Lesson 2: Meditation for Emotional Regulation

Lesson 2:
Meditation for Emotional Regulation

Using Meditation for Emotional Regulation: A Journey to Inner Peace

In the heart of Goodness, Strategy Middle/High School was known for its supportive and nurturing environment. Among the dedicated teachers was Mrs. Regulate, who led the Learning Strategies class. She had a unique talent for helping students manage their emotions and find inner peace.

The Challenge

Nia, Lenny, and Ahlani were three students in Mrs. Regulate's class. Each faced unique challenges with emotional regulation. Nia often felt overwhelmed by her emotions and struggled to stay calm. Lenny had a fiery temper that sometimes got him into trouble, and Ahlani found it challenging to cope with anxiety and stress.

One sunny morning, Mrs. Regulate gathered her students for an important lesson. "Today, we're going to learn about the power of meditation for emotional regulation," she announced. "Meditation can help you manage your emotions, stay calm, and find inner peace."

The Introduction to Meditation for Emotional Regulation

Mrs. Regulate began by explaining the basics of meditation. "Meditation helps train your mind to stay present and focused. By practicing regularly, you can learn to control your emotions and respond to situations calmly."

Nia raised her hand. "How can meditation help us stay calm when feeling overwhelmed, Mrs. Regulate?"

"Great question, Nia," Mrs. Regulate replied. "Let's explore some specific techniques that can help."

Mindful Breathing for Nia

Mrs. Regulate guided the class through a simple mindful breathing exercise. "Sit comfortably, close your eyes, and focus on your breath. Take a deep breath in for four counts, hold it for four, and breathe out for four."

Nia followed along, feeling her mind clear with each breath. "When you feel overwhelmed by emotions, take a few minutes to practice mindful breathing," Mrs. Regulate suggested. "It will help calm your mind and body."

Positive Visualization for Lenny

Next, Mrs. Regulate introduced positive visualization. "Close your eyes and imagine yourself in a peaceful place, like a beach or a quiet forest," she instructed.

Lenny closed his eyes and visualized himself sitting by a calm lake, feeling the warmth of the sun and the gentle breeze. "By visualizing a peaceful place, you can train your mind to stay calm and relaxed," Mrs. Regulate explained. "This can help you manage your temper and respond to situations more calmly."

Mantra Repetition for Ahlani

Mrs. Regulate then taught the class about mantra repetition. "Choose a calming word or phrase, like 'peace' or 'I am calm,' and repeat it silently while you breathe."

Ahlani chose the mantra "I am calm." As she repeated it, she felt her anxiety begin to fade. "Using a mantra can help anchor your mind and reduce anxiety," Mrs. Regulate said. "It's a powerful way to maintain emotional balance."

Integrating Meditation into Daily Life

Mrs. Regulate emphasized the importance of integrating meditation into daily routines. "Consistency is key," she said. "Set aside a specific time each day to practice these techniques. Whether it's in the morning, during a break, or before bed, regular practice will help you manage your emotions more effectively."

The Transformation

As the weeks passed, Nia, Lenny, and Ahlani diligently practiced meditation techniques. Nia used mindful breathing to stay calm when she felt overwhelmed, Lenny visualized peaceful places to manage his temper, and Ahlani repeated her mantra to cope with anxiety.

They soon noticed significant improvements. Nia felt more in control of her emotions, Lenny responded to situations more calmly, and Ahlani found it easier to manage stress. Their overall well-being improved, and they felt more confident handling challenging situations.

Conclusion

One day, Mrs. Regulate asked her students to reflect on their experiences. "How has using meditation for emotional regulation helped you?"

Nia smiled. "Mindful breathing helps me stay calm when I'm feeling overwhelmed. I don't feel as out of control anymore."

Lenny nodded. "Positive visualization helps me manage my temper. I can respond to situations more calmly now."

Ahlani added, "Repeating my mantra keeps me centered and calm. I feel less anxious and more in control."

Mrs. Regulate beamed with pride. "I'm glad to hear that meditation is helping you. Remember, the key to success is consistency. Keep practicing, and you'll continue to see improvements."

The students of Strategy Middle/High School realized that meditation was not just a tool for relaxation but a powerful practice for emotional regulation. With Mrs. Regulate's guidance, they learned to apply meditation to their daily lives, unlocking their full potential and paving the way for a brighter, more peaceful future.

Week 8: Advanced Meditation Techniques

Lesson 1:
Visualization and Guided Imagery

Exploring Advanced Meditation Techniques: Visualization and Guided Imagery

At Strategy Middle/High School, students were encouraged to explore innovative ways to enhance their learning and personal growth. Ms. Advance, the Learning Strategies teacher, was known for introducing advanced techniques to help students excel. Her class was a haven for students seeking to deepen their understanding and practice of meditation.

The Introduction to Advanced Techniques

Na'ima, Naudia, and Nyrie were three students in Ms. Advance's class. Each faced unique challenges and was eager to find new ways to overcome them. Na'ima struggled with staying focused on her goals, Naudia often felt overwhelmed by stress, and Nyrie had difficulty visualizing success in his endeavors.

One sunny morning, Ms. Advance gathered her students for an important lesson. "Today, we're going to explore advanced meditation techniques: visualization and guided imagery," she announced. "These techniques can help you improve focus, manage stress, and achieve your goals."

Visualization for Na'ima

Ms. Advance began by explaining the concept of visualization. "Visualization is a technique where you create a mental image of achieving a specific goal. It helps you stay focused and motivated."

Na'ima raised her hand. "How can visualization help me focus on my goals, Ms. Advance?"

"Great question, Na'ima," Ms. Advance replied. "Let's practice together. Close your eyes and imagine yourself achieving one of your goals. See yourself taking the necessary steps, overcoming obstacles, and finally reaching your goal. Feel the pride and joy of your accomplishment."

Na'ima closed her eyes and visualized herself finishing her science project on time and presenting it confidently to the class. She saw herself working diligently, staying organized, and receiving praise from her teacher. This vivid image motivated her to stay focused and work towards her goal.

Guided Imagery for Naudia

Next, Ms. Advance introduced guided imagery. "Guided imagery involves using detailed mental images to create a relaxing and positive experience. It's beneficial for managing stress."

Naudia looked intrigued. "How do we use guided imagery to manage stress?"

"Let's try it together," Ms. Advance suggested. "Close your eyes and imagine a place where you feel completely relaxed and safe. It could be a beach, a forest, or anywhere that brings you peace. Imagine all the details: the sounds, the smells, the colors. Allow yourself to fully immerse yourself in this peaceful place."

Naudia closed her eyes and imagined herself sitting by a tranquil lake, listening to the gentle water lapping and feeling the sun's warmth on her skin. She felt her stress melt away as she focused on the serene imagery. This practice helped her manage stress and find a sense of calm during difficult times.

Combining Techniques for Nyrie

Ms. Advance then turned to Nyrie. "Nyrie, let's combine both techniques. Visualization can help you see your success, and guided imagery can provide the relaxation you need to achieve it."

Nyrie nodded. "How do I start, Ms. Advance?"

"Close your eyes and start with guided imagery," Ms. Advance instructed. "Imagine a peaceful place where you feel relaxed and safe. Once fully immersed in this place, visualize yourself succeeding in a specific task or goal."

Nyrie closed his eyes and imagined himself in a quiet forest surrounded by tall trees and the sound of birds chirping. As he felt relaxed and centered, he began to visualize himself performing well in his upcoming soccer game. He saw himself making precise passes, scoring goals, and leading his team to victory. This combination of techniques boosted his confidence and helped him prepare mentally for the game.

The Transformation

As the weeks passed, Na'ima, Naudia, and Nyrie diligently practiced their advanced meditation techniques. Na'ima used visualization to stay focused on her goals, Naudia practiced guided imagery to manage stress, and Nyrie combined both methods to enhance his performance and confidence.

They soon noticed significant improvements. Na'ima felt more motivated and organized, Naudia experienced less stress and calmness, and Nyrie felt more confident and prepared for challenges. Their well-being improved, and they felt more empowered to achieve their goals.

Conclusion

One day, Ms. Advance asked her students to reflect on their experiences. "How have these advanced meditation techniques helped you?"

Na'ima smiled. "Visualization helps me stay focused on my goals. I feel more motivated and confident."

Naudia nodded. "Guided imagery helps me manage stress and find peace. I feel more relaxed and in control."

Nyrie added, "Combining both techniques boosts my confidence and performance. I feel more prepared for challenges."

Ms. Advance beamed with pride. "I'm glad to hear that these techniques are helping you. Remember, the key to success is practice and consistency. Keep applying these techniques, and you'll see positive changes."

The Strategy Middle/High School students realized that advanced meditation techniques were powerful tools for achieving success and well-being. With Ms. Advance's guidance, they learned to apply visualization and guided imagery to their daily lives, unlocking their full potential and paving the way for a brighter future.

Lesson 2: Meditation and Self-Compassion

Lesson 2:
Meditation and Self-Compassion

The Power of Meditation and Self-Compassion

At Strategy Middle/High School, students were always encouraged to explore innovative ways to improve their academic performance and personal well-being. Mr. Compassion, the Learning Strategies teacher, was mainly known for his empathetic approach and dedication to teaching students about the importance of self-compassion and mindfulness.

The Challenge

Noah, Kenlyn, and Mason were three students in Mr. Compassion's class. Each faced unique challenges. Noah often felt overwhelmed by his perfectionism, Kenlyn struggled with self-doubt, and Mason struggled with failure and setbacks.

One bright morning, Mr. Compassion gathered his students for an important lesson. "Today, we're going to learn about the power of meditation and self-compassion," he announced. "These practices can help you manage stress, build resilience, and improve your overall well-being."

The Introduction to Meditation and Self-Compassion

Mr. Compassion began by explaining the concepts. "Self-compassion means being kind to yourself, especially during difficult times. It involves recognizing that everyone makes mistakes and faces challenges. Meditation helps us become more aware of our thoughts and feelings, allowing us to respond with compassion rather than criticism."

Noah raised his hand. "How can meditation help us be more compassionate to ourselves, Mr. Compassion?"

"Great question, Noah," Mr. Compassion replied. "Let's explore some specific techniques that can help."

Mindful Breathing for Noah

Mr. Compassion guided the class through a simple mindful breathing exercise. "Sit comfortably, close your eyes, and focus on your breath. Take a deep breath in for four counts, hold it for four, and breathe out for four."

Noah followed along, feeling his mind clear with each breath. "When you feel overwhelmed by perfectionism, take a few minutes to practice mindful breathing," Mr. Compassion suggested. "It will help calm your mind and allow you to approach your tasks more kindly and with less pressure."

Loving-Kindness Meditation for Kenlyn

Next, Mr. Compassion introduced loving-kindness meditation. "This technique involves sending kind thoughts to yourself and others. Close your eyes and think of someone you care about. Silently repeat the phrases, 'May you be happy, may you be healthy, may you be safe, may you live with ease.' Then, direct these phrases toward yourself."

Kenlyn closed her eyes and followed the instructions. She felt a sense of warmth and compassion as she repeated the phrases. "By practicing loving-kindness meditation, you can build self-compassion and reduce self-doubt," Mr. Compassion explained. "It helps you treat yourself with the same kindness you would offer to a friend."

Self-Compassion Break for Mason

Mr. Compassion then taught the class about the self-compassion break. "Whenever you face a difficult situation, take a self-compassion break. Place your hand on your heart, acknowledge your feelings, and say, 'This is a moment of suffering. Suffering is a part of life. May I be kind to myself in this moment.'"

Mason placed his hand on his heart and repeated the phrases. He felt a sense of comfort and understanding. "Using the self-compassion break can help you cope with failure and setbacks more effectively," Mr. Compassion said. "It reminds you that it's okay to make mistakes and that you deserve kindness and support."

Integrating Practices into Daily Life

Mr. Compassion emphasized the importance of integrating these practices into daily routines. "Consistency is key," he said. "Set aside time each day to practice mindfulness and self-compassion. Whether it's in the morning, during a break, or before bed, regular practice will help you build resilience and well-being."

The Transformation

As the weeks passed, Noah, Kenlyn, and Mason diligently practiced meditation and self-compassion techniques. Noah used mindful breathing to manage his perfectionism, Kenlyn practiced loving-kindness meditation to reduce self-doubt, and Mason took self-compassion breaks to cope with setbacks.

They soon noticed significant improvements. Noah felt more relaxed and less pressured, Kenlyn experienced increased self-confidence, and Mason felt more resilient in facing challenges. Their overall well-being improved, and they felt more empowered to navigate their academic and personal lives.

Conclusion

One day, Mr. Compassion asked his students to reflect on their experiences. "How have meditation and self-compassion helped you?"

Noah smiled. "Mindful breathing helps me stay calm and approach my tasks with kindness. I don't feel as overwhelmed anymore."

Kenlyn nodded. "Loving-kindness meditation has increased my self-confidence. I treat myself with more compassion now."

Mason added, "The self-compassion break helps me cope with setbacks. I feel more resilient and supported."

Mr. Compassion beamed with pride. "I'm glad to hear that these practices are helping you. Remember, the key to success is practice and consistency. Keep applying these techniques, and you'll see positive changes."

The Strategy Middle/High School students realized that meditation and self-compassion were powerful tools for enhancing their well-being and achieving success. With Mr. Compassion's guidance, they learned to apply these practices to their daily lives, unlocking their full potential and paving the way for a brighter, more compassionate future.

Week 9: Integrating Meditation with Learning

Lesson 1: Mindful Study Practices

Integrating Meditation with Learning: The Mindful Study Practice

At Strategy Middle/High School, students constantly explored innovative ways to enhance their learning experience and personal growth. Mr. Mindful, the Learning Strategies teacher, was renowned for his ability to teach students how to integrate meditation into their study practices to improve focus, retention, and overall academic performance.

The Challenge

Mason, Noah, Nyrie, Kenlyn, Ahlani, and Nia were all students in Mr. Mindful's class, each with unique academic challenges. Mason needed help concentrating during long study sessions. Noah often felt anxious before exams. Nyrie needed help with retaining information. Kenlyn needed help staying organized. Ahlani frequently felt overwhelmed by her workload, and Nia struggled to balance her schoolwork and extracurricular activities.

One bright morning, Mr. Mindful gathered his students for an important lesson. "Today, we're going to learn about the importance of integrating meditation with learning," he announced. "This mindful study practice can help you focus better, retain information, and reduce stress."

The Introduction to Mindful Study Practice

Mr. Mindful began by explaining the concept. "Mindful study practice involves using meditation techniques to enhance your learning. It helps you stay present, calm, and focused while studying, which can significantly improve your academic performance."

Mason raised his hand. "How can meditation help us study better, Mr. Mindful?"

"Great question, Mason," Mr. Mindful replied. "Let's explore some specific techniques that can help."

Mindful Breathing for Focus

Mr. Mindful guided the class through a simple mindful breathing exercise. "Sit comfortably, close your eyes, and focus on your breath. Take a deep breath in for four counts, hold it for four, and breathe out for four."

Mason followed along, feeling his mind clear with each breath. "When you feel distracted or overwhelmed during your study sessions, take a few minutes to practice mindful breathing," Mr. Mindful suggested. "It will help you refocus and calm your mind."

Body Scan for Relaxation

Next, Mr. Mindful introduced the body scan technique. "This practice helps you relax and become aware of your body. Sit comfortably, close your eyes, and focus on each part of your body, starting from your toes and moving up to your head. Relax each part as you go along."

Noah closed his eyes and followed the instructions. As he relaxed each part of his body, his anxiety faded. "Using the body scan technique before an exam can help you stay calm and focused," Mr. Mindful explained.

Visualization for Retention

Mr. Mindful then taught the class about visualization. "This technique involves creating a mental image of what you're studying. Close your eyes and imagine the information as vividly as possible."

Nyrie visualized himself reading his history textbook and seeing the key events and dates come to life in his mind. "Visualization helps improve retention by making the information more memorable," Mr. Mindful said.

Mantra Repetition for Organization

"Kenlyn, let's try mantra repetition to help you stay organized," Mr. Mindful suggested. "Choose a calming word or phrase, like 'focus' or 'I am organized,' and repeat it silently while you study."

Kenlyn chose the mantra "I am focused." As she repeated it, she felt more centered and less overwhelmed by her tasks. "Using a mantra can help you stay on track and manage your study time effectively," Mr. Mindful explained.

Guided Imagery for Stress Reduction

"Ahlani, let's practice guided imagery to help you manage stress," Mr. Mindful continued. "Close your eyes and imagine a peaceful place where you feel completely relaxed. Focus on the details and let the imagery calm your mind."

Ahlani imagined herself sitting by a tranquil lake, feeling the sun's warmth and hearing the gentle lapping of the water. This practice helped her feel more balanced and less stressed about her workload.

Integrating Practices into Daily Routine

"Nia, let's discuss balancing schoolwork with extracurricular activities using these techniques," Mr. Mindful said. "Incorporate mindful study practices into your daily routine. Set aside specific times for studying and activities, and use meditation techniques to stay focused and relaxed."

Nia nodded, understanding how to create a balanced schedule that included her schoolwork and activities.

The Transformation

As the weeks passed, Mason, Noah, Nyrie, Kenlyn, Ahlani, and Nia diligently practiced their mindful study techniques. Mason used mindful breathing to stay focused during study sessions, Noah practiced the body scan to calm his exam anxiety, Nyrie used visualization to improve retention, Kenlyn repeated her mantra to keep organized, Ahlani practiced guided imagery to manage stress, and Nia balanced her schedule with mindful study practices.

They soon noticed significant improvements. Mason found it easier to concentrate, Noah felt less anxious before exams, Nyrie remembered information better, Kenlyn managed her tasks more effectively, Ahlani felt more balanced, and Nia successfully balanced her schoolwork and activities.

Conclusion

One day, Mr. Mindful asked his students to reflect on their experiences. "How have mindful study practices helped you?"

Mason smiled. "Mindful breathing helps me stay focused. I don't get distracted as easily anymore."

Noah nodded. "The body scan technique calms my exam anxiety. I feel more relaxed and ready."

Nyrie added, "Visualization helps me remember information better. It's like the material comes to life."

Kenlyn said, "Repeating my mantra keeps me organized and focused. It helps me manage my study time better."

Ahlani agreed. "Guided imagery helps me reduce stress. I feel more balanced."

Nia concluded, "Incorporating these practices into my routine has helped me balance my schoolwork and activities. I feel more in control."

Mr. Mindful beamed with pride. "I'm glad to hear that these techniques are helping you. Remember, the key to success is practice and consistency. You'll see positive changes by applying these mindful study practices."

The Strategy Middle/High School students realized that integrating meditation with learning was a powerful way to enhance their academic performance and personal well-being. With Mr. Mindful's guidance, they learned to apply these practices to their daily lives, unlocking their full potential and paving the way for a brighter future.

Lesson 2: Reflection and Meditation

Lesson 2:
Reflection and Meditation

The Importance of Reflection and Meditation

At Strategy Middle/High School, students were always encouraged to find ways to improve their learning and personal growth. Mrs. Reflection, the Learning Strategies teacher, was known for her emphasis on the power of reflection and meditation. She believed these practices were essential for students to gain insight into their thoughts and emotions, leading to better academic performance and overall well-being.

The Challenge

Na'ima, Naudia, Kimiyah, Levi, Nilan, and Lenny were all students in Mrs. Reflection's class. Each faced unique challenges. Na'ima struggled with staying focused on her goals, Naudia often felt overwhelmed by stress, Kimiyah had difficulty balancing her schoolwork with extracurricular activities, Levi struggled to manage his time effectively, Nilan struggled with self-confidence, and Lenny had trouble dealing with his emotions.

One sunny morning, Mrs. Reflection gathered her students for an important lesson. "Today, we're going to learn about the importance of reflection and meditation," she announced. "These practices can help you better understand your thoughts and emotions, leading to improved focus, reduced stress, and greater overall well-being."

The Introduction to Reflection and Meditation

Mrs. Reflection began by explaining the concepts. "Reflection involves taking time to think about your experiences, thoughts, and emotions. Meditation helps you become more aware of your present moment, allowing you to respond to situations more clearly and calmly."

Na'ima raised her hand. "How can reflection and meditation help us with our schoolwork, Mrs. Reflection?"

"Great question, Na'ima," Mrs. Reflection replied. "Let's explore some specific techniques that can help."

Journaling for Reflection

Mrs. Reflection guided the class through a journaling exercise. "Take out your notebooks and write about a recent experience that challenged you. Reflect on what happened, how you felt, and what you learned from it."

Naudia wrote about a stressful project she had recently completed. As she reflected on her experience, she realized that her stress was due to poor time management and that she could improve by planning better in the future. "Journaling helps you gain insights into your experiences and learn from them," Mrs. Reflection explained.

Mindful Breathing for Meditation

Next, Mrs. Reflection introduced mindful breathing. "Sit comfortably, close your eyes, and focus on your breath. Take a deep breath in for four counts, hold it for four, and breathe out for four."

Kimiyah followed along, feeling her mind clear with each breath. "Mindful breathing helps you stay present and calm, reducing stress and improving focus," Mrs. Reflection said.

Visualization for Goal Setting

Mrs. Reflection then taught the class about visualization. "Close your eyes and imagine yourself achieving a specific goal. See yourself taking the necessary steps and overcoming obstacles."

Levi visualized himself managing his time effectively, completing his assignments on time, and still having time for his hobbies. "Visualization helps you stay focused and motivated," Mrs. Reflection explained.

Body Scan for Relaxation

"Nilan, let's try a body scan to help you relax and build self-confidence," Mrs. Reflection suggested. "Sit comfortably, close your eyes, and focus on each part of your body, starting from your toes and moving up to your head. Relax each part as you go along."

Nilan closed his eyes and followed the instructions. As he relaxed each body part, he felt his self-confidence grow. "The body scan technique helps you become aware of your body and reduce tension," Mrs. Reflection said.

Loving-Kindness Meditation for Emotional Regulation

"Lenny, let's practice loving-kindness meditation to help you manage your emotions," Mrs. Reflection continued. "Close your eyes and think of someone you care about. Silently repeat the phrases, 'May you be happy, may you be healthy, may you be safe, may you live with ease.' Then, direct these phrases toward yourself."

Lenny followed along and felt a sense of warmth and compassion. "Loving-kindness meditation helps you develop self-compassion and emotional balance," Mrs. Reflection explained.

Integrating Practices into Daily Routine

"Na'ima, let's discuss how to integrate these practices into your daily routine," Mrs. Reflection said. "Set aside time each day for reflection and meditation. Whether it's in the morning, during a break, or before bed, regular practice will help you gain insights and maintain well-being."

Na'ima nodded, understanding how to create a balanced routine that included time for reflection and meditation.

The Transformation

As the weeks passed, Na'ima, Naudia, Kimiyah, Levi, Nilan, and Lenny diligently practiced reflection and meditation techniques. Na'ima used journaling to stay focused on her goals, Naudia practiced mindful breathing to reduce stress, Kimiyah balanced her schedule with visualization, Levi managed his time better with body scans, Nilan built self-confidence through body scans, and Lenny worked his emotions with loving-kindness meditation.

They soon noticed significant improvements. Na'ima felt more focused and motivated, Naudia experienced less stress, Kimiyah balanced her schoolwork and activities, Levi managed his time effectively, Nilan felt more confident, and Lenny had better emotional control.

Conclusion

One day, Mrs. Reflection asked her students to reflect on their experiences. "How have reflection and meditation helped you?"

Na'ima smiled. "Journaling helps me stay focused on my goals. I can see my progress and what I need to improve."

Naudia nodded. "Mindful breathing reduces my stress. I feel more present and calm."

Kimiyah added, "Visualization helps me balance my schedule. I stay motivated and on track."

Levi said, "Body scans help me manage my time. I feel more organized."

Nilan agreed. "Body scans build my self-confidence. I feel more relaxed."

Lenny concluded, "Loving-kindness meditation helps me manage my emotions. I feel more balanced."

Mrs. Reflection beamed with pride. "I'm glad to hear that these practices are helping you. Remember, the key to success is practice and consistency. Keep applying these techniques, and you'll see positive changes."

The Strategy Middle/High School students realized that reflection and meditation were powerful tools for enhancing their academic performance and personal well-being. With Mrs. Reflection's guidance, they learned to apply these practices to their daily lives, unlocking their full potential and paving the way for a brighter future.

Unit 3:

The Superpower of Executive Functioning Skills (Weeks 10-15)

Week 10: Introduction to Executive Functioning

Lesson 1:
What are Executive Functioning Skills?

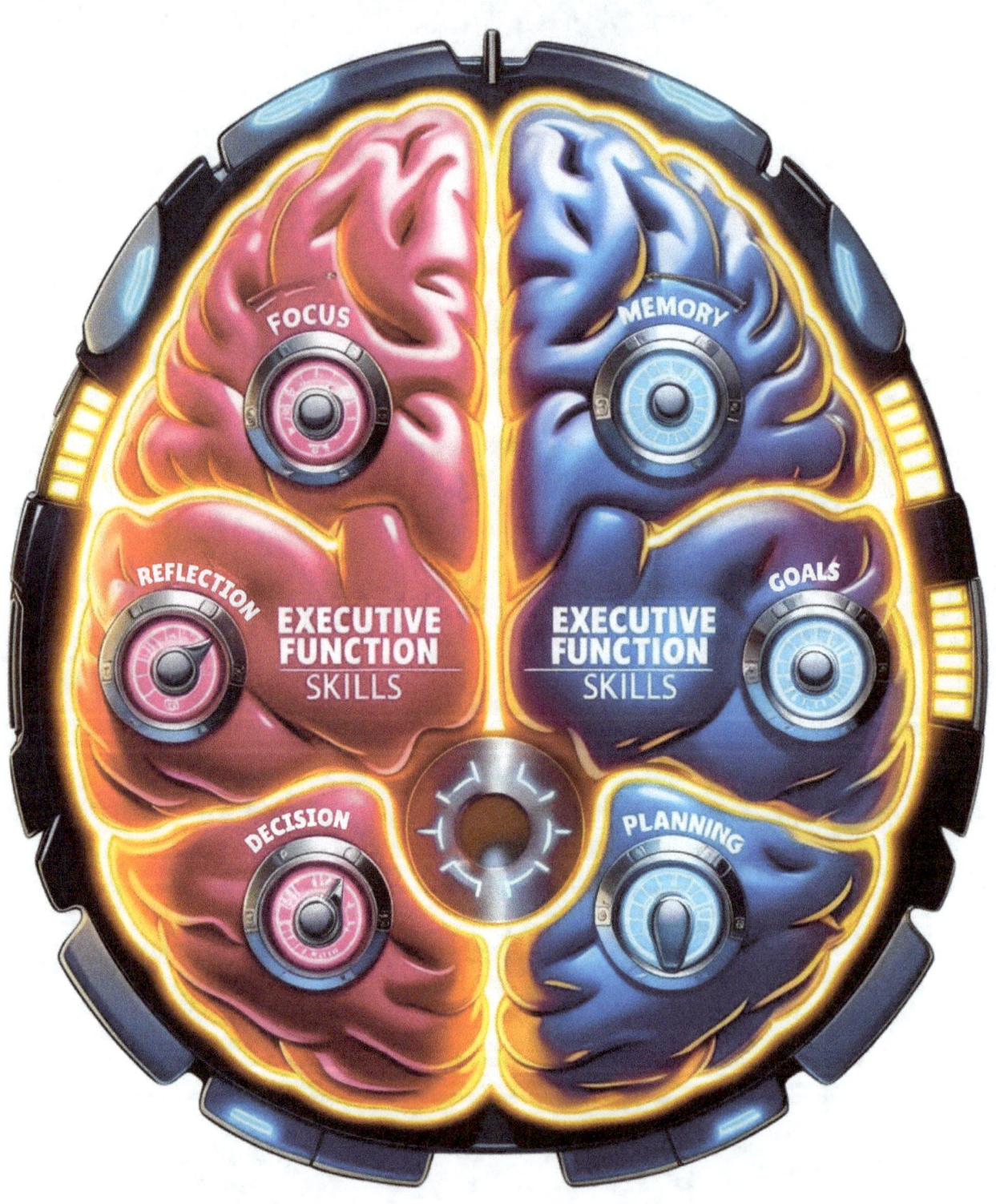

Lesson 1: What are Executive Functioning Skills?

The Superpower of Executive Functioning Skills

In the lively town of Goodness, nestled in a valley surrounded by lush greenery, Strategy Middle/High School stood as a beacon of learning and growth. Inside its bright, bustling halls, students learned to unlock their hidden potential, none more so than in Mr. Executive's class. Mr. Executive was the learning strategies teacher, known for his wisdom and kind heart. He was on a mission to help his students discover their inner superpowers by mastering executive functioning skills.

His class included six special students: Kimiyah, Naudia, Na'ima, Noah, Mason, and Levi. Each of them faced unique academic challenges that made school a bit tougher. Mr. Executive knew that with the right tools, they could turn their struggles into strengths.

One sunny morning, Mr. Executive gathered his students and began, "Today, we will learn about something powerful—executive functioning skills. These skills are like the brain's control center. They help us plan, organize, remember instructions, and manage our time."

He wrote on the board:

1. **Planning** - Making a roadmap to reach a goal.

2. **Organization** - Keeping track of things physically and mentally.

3. **Time Management** - Using time wisely to get things done.

4. **Memory** - Keeping important information in mind.

5. **Focus** - Staying on task and avoiding distractions.

6. **Problem-solving** - Finding solutions when things get tough.

"These skills are essential for success," he continued. "They help us in all subjects, at home, and even in the office."

Kimiyah, a bright and creative student, often found herself overwhelmed with long-term projects. She struggled to break them down into manageable steps.

Mr. Executive sat with her and said, "Kimiyah, planning is like creating a map. Let's break your project into smaller tasks and set deadlines for each."

Kimiyah's eyes lit up as they created a step-by-step plan. Over time, she began to see her projects as achievable journeys rather than insurmountable mountains.

Naudia was constantly losing her homework and forgetting where she placed essential papers. She found her backpack a chaotic mess.

Mr. Executive introduced her to organizational tools like color-coded folders and a checklist system. "By organizing your materials, you'll always know where to find what you need," he explained.

Naudia started using these tools and noticed that keeping track of her assignments and notes was much more accessible.

Na'ima often procrastinated and rushed through assignments at the last minute. She struggled with effectively managing her time.

"Time management is key, Na'ima," Mr. Executive said. "Let's create a daily schedule that balances schoolwork with breaks and fun activities."

With a clear schedule, Na'ima learned to prioritize her tasks and found she had more time for what she enjoyed.

Noah had a hard time remembering instructions and essential details from his lessons.

Mr. Executive taught him mnemonic devices and the art of note-taking. "By using these techniques, you'll be able to remember and recall information more easily," he assured Noah.

Noah started using visual aids and memory tricks, and soon, he noticed an improvement in his ability to retain information.

Mason was easily distracted in class and needed help staying on task.

"Focus is like a muscle that needs training," Mr. Executive said. He introduced Mason to mindfulness exercises and techniques to minimize distractions.

With practice, Mason began to stay on task longer and found his concentration improving during lessons.

Levi often felt stuck when encountering complex problems and didn't know how to proceed.

Mr. Executive encouraged Levi to approach problems step-by-step, asking questions like, "What do I know?" and "What do I need to find out?"

By breaking problems down and tackling them systematically, Levi gained confidence and improved his problem-solving skills.

As the days passed, Kimiyah, Naudia, Na'ima, Noah, Mason, and Levi began to notice changes in their academic performance. They felt more confident, capable, and ready to tackle any challenge. Mr. Executive's teachings showed them that executive functioning skills were their superpowers.

"Remember," Mr. Executive said one day, "these skills will help you in school, at home, and any future career you choose. You've all done amazing work, and I'm so proud of each of you."

The students beamed with pride, knowing they had the tools to succeed, no matter where life took them. With their newfound superpowers, they were ready to take on the world.

Lesson 2:
Assessing Your Executive Functioning Skills

Assessing Your Executive Functioning Skills

In the bustling town of Goodness, Strategy Middle/High School was known for nurturing its students' unique strengths and abilities. Among the dedicated teachers at the school, Ms. Assess stood out for her expertise in helping students understand and improve their executive functioning skills.

Ms. Assess had a particular group of students in her class: Levi, Nilan, Nyrie, Nia, Ahlani, and Kenlyn. Each had heard about executive functioning skills but didn't quite understand how to assess their abilities.

One sunny morning, Ms. Assess gathered her students and said, "Today, we will learn how to assess our executive functioning skills. We can develop strategies to enhance our learning by understanding where we are strong and where we need improvement."

She wrote on the board: "Assessing Your Executive Functioning Skills."

She continued, "Executive functioning skills include planning, organization, time management, memory, focus, and problem-solving. Let's explore each one and see how you can assess yourselves."

Planning

Ms. Assess began with planning. "Planning is about making a roadmap to reach a goal. To assess your planning skills, ask yourself:

- Can I break down a big task into smaller steps?
- Do I set goals and make a plan to achieve them?"

Levi raised his hand, "Sometimes I start a project but get stuck because I don't know the next steps."

Ms. Assess smiled, "That's a good insight, Levi. Knowing where you need help is the first step in improving."

Organization

Next, Ms. Assess moved on to organization. "Organization means keeping track of things physically and mentally. Ask yourselves:

- Do I keep my workspace and materials organized?
- Can I find my assignments and notes easily?"

Nyrie nodded, "My backpack is always a mess, and I lose things often."

"That's a common challenge, Nyrie," Ms. Assess said. "We'll work on strategies to improve that."

Time Management

Ms. Assess then talked about time management. "Time management is using your time wisely to get things done. Consider:

- Do I finish my tasks on time?
- Can I estimate how long a task will take and plan accordingly?"

Nia looked thoughtful, "I usually underestimate how long my homework will take, and then I'm rushed."

Ms. Assess nodded, "Recognizing that helps us find better ways to manage time."

Memory

Moving on to memory, Ms. Assess explained, "Memory involves keeping important information in mind. Reflect on:

- Do I remember instructions and details from my lessons?
- Can I recall information when I need it?"

Kenlyn sighed, "I often forget what the teacher said in class."

"That's okay, Kenlyn," Ms. Assess reassured. "We'll practice some memory techniques."

Focus

Next was focus. "Focus is about staying on task and avoiding distractions. Think about:

- Can I concentrate on my work without getting distracted?
- Do I stay on task until I'm finished?"

Ahlani admitted, "I get distracted easily, especially when doing homework."

"Many students face that challenge, Ahlani," Ms. Assess said. "We can work on ways to improve your focus."

Problem-Solving

Finally, Ms. Assess addressed problem-solving. "Problem-solving is finding solutions when things get tough. Ask yourselves:

- Can I think of different ways to solve a problem?
- Do I stay calm and try again if my first solution doesn't work?"

Nilan said, "I get frustrated when I can't solve a problem immediately."

"Understanding that frustration is normal is important, Nilan," Ms. Assess said. "We'll learn how to tackle problems step-by-step."

Self-Assessment Activity

Ms. Assess handed out a worksheet to each student titled "Assessing My Executive Functioning Skills." The worksheet had questions for each skill area, prompting students to reflect on their strengths and areas for improvement.

"Take your time and answer these questions honestly," she instructed. "This will help us create a plan to enhance your executive functioning skills."

The students spent the subsequent few minutes thoughtfully filling out their worksheets. Ms. Assess walked around the room as they worked, offering encouragement and answering questions.

Reflection and Goal Setting

Once everyone finished, Ms. Assess gathered the class. "Now that you've assessed your skills, think about one area in which you want to improve. Write down a specific goal and one strategy to achieve it."

Levi wrote, "I will improve my planning by breaking down projects into smaller tasks and setting deadlines."

Nyrie said, "I will organize my backpack using color-coded folders."

Nia planned, "I will manage my time better by creating a homework schedule."

Kenlyn said, "I will use mnemonic devices to help remember instructions."

Ahlani chose, "I will practice mindfulness exercises to improve my focus."

Nilan set his goal, "I will stay calm and try different solutions when solving problems."

Conclusion

Ms. Assess beamed with pride as she saw the determination in her students' eyes. "You've all taken an important step in understanding your executive functioning skills. By setting these goals, you're on your way to becoming even more successful learners."

The students left the classroom feeling empowered and ready to tackle their academic challenges with newfound strategies and confidence. They knew that with Ms. Assess's guidance, they could unlock their full potential and excel in all areas of their lives.

Week 11: Developing Planning and Organization Skills

Lesson 1: Creating Effective Study Plans

Lesson 1: Creating Effective Study Plans

Developing Planning and Organization Skills: Creating Effective Study Plans

In the bustling town of Goodness, Strategy Middle/High School was where students discovered their strengths and worked on their weaknesses. Among the various classes, Mr. Executive's was particularly special. Known for his wisdom and kind heart, he focused on teaching students the vital skills to succeed in school and life.

One day, Mr. Executive gathered his students—Noah, Kenlyn, Mason, Lenny, Nia, and Ahlani—for an important lesson on developing planning and organization skills, specifically creating effective study plans.

"Today," Mr. Executive began, "we're going to learn how to make study plans that will help you stay organized and make your studying more effective. These skills will help you in school and other areas of your life."

He noticed his students' eager but slightly puzzled faces and continued, "Let's start with planning."

Planning

"Planning," Mr. Executive explained, "is about making a roadmap to reach your goals. When it comes to studying, planning helps you know what you need to do and when you need to do it."

He wrote on the board: "1. Set Goals, 2. Break Down Tasks, 3. Set Deadlines."

"First," he said, "you must set clear goals. What do you want to achieve? For example, let's say you have a math test in two weeks. Your goal might be to understand all the chapters on the test."

Noah raised his hand, "How do we break down tasks, Mr. Executive?"

"Good question, Noah," Mr. Executive replied. "Once you have your goal, you divide it into smaller tasks. For your math test, you might list the chapters you need to study, the problems you need to practice, and the time you need to review your notes."

Kenlyn nodded, "And then we set deadlines for each task?"

"Exactly," Mr. Executive affirmed. Set realistic deadlines for each task to ensure you stay on track."

Organization

Next, Mr. Executive moved on to the organization. "Organization is about keeping everything in its place so you can find it easily when needed."

He wrote on the board: "1. Organize Materials, 2. Use Tools, 3. Keep Track."

"First," he said, "organize your study materials. Use folders, binders, or digital tools to organize your notes and assignments. For example, use a different folder for each subject."

Mason chimed in, "What tools can we use?"

"There are many tools you can use," Mr. Executive said. "Planners, calendars, apps, and checklists can help you keep track of your tasks and deadlines."

Nia looked thoughtful, "And how do we keep track of our progress?"

"Great point, Nia," Mr. Executive said. "Keep track of your progress by regularly checking off tasks as you complete them. This helps you stay organized and gives you a sense of accomplishment."

Creating a Study Plan

"Now," Mr. Executive continued, "let's create a study plan together. We'll use the math test example."

He drew a simple table on the board with columns for "Task," "Deadline," and "Completed."

Task	Deadline	Completed
Chapter 1 Notes	Day 1	
Practice Problems Chapter 1	Day 2	
Chapter 2 Notes	Day 3	
Practice Problems Chapter 2	Day 4	
Review Chapters 1 and 2	Day 5	

"Let's fill this out together," Mr. Executive said. "What should our first task be?"

"Chapter 1 Notes," Lenny suggested.

"Good start," Mr. Executive said, writing it down. "And the deadline?"

"Day 1," Ahlani added.

They continued filling the table, breaking the study plan into manageable tasks with clear deadlines.

Reflection and Application

After completing the study plan, Mr. Executive turned to his students. "Now that we have a plan, how do you feel about studying for the math test?"

Kenlyn smiled, "It feels less overwhelming."

"Exactly," Mr. Executive said. "A good plan makes a big task feel manageable. Remember, the key is to stay organized and stick to your plan."

He handed out blank study plan templates to each student. "I want you to create your study plan for an upcoming test or project. Use what we've learned today and see how it helps you."

The students eagerly took the templates and started working on their plans, feeling more confident and prepared.

Conclusion

As the class ended, Mr. Executive reminded them, "Planning and organization are powerful skills that will help you in many areas of your life. Keep practicing, and you'll see great results."

The students left the classroom with newfound control over their studies. They knew that with adequate planning and organization, they could tackle any academic challenge that came their way.

Lesson 2: Organizing Materials and Space

Lesson 2:
Organizing Materials and Space

Organizing Materials and Space: A Journey to a Tidy Mind

In the vibrant town of Goodness, Strategy Middle/High School was known for nurturing academic excellence and essential life skills. One of the most beloved teachers, Ms. Order, was renowned for her ability to help students organize their materials and spaces, which she believed was crucial for a clear and focused mind.

Ms. Order's class included Na'ima, Naudia, Kimiyah, Nyrie, Lenny, and Noah. Each student had a unique style but needed help keeping their materials and spaces organized. One sunny afternoon, Ms. Order decided it was time to help her students master the art of organization.

"Good afternoon, everyone!" Ms. Order greeted with a warm smile. "Today, we're going to embark on a journey to learn how organizing our materials and spaces can help us succeed more in school and life."

The students exchanged curious glances, intrigued by what Ms. Order had planned.

Understanding Organization

Ms. Order began, "Organization means keeping things in order so you can find them easily and stay focused on your tasks. Let's break it down into two parts: organizing your materials and space."

She wrote on the board:

1. **Organizing Materials**

    - Use folders and binders
    - Label everything
    - Keep a checklist

2. **Organizing Space**
   - Keep your desk tidy
   - Create designated areas for items
   - Minimize distractions

Organizing Materials

"First, let's talk about organizing materials," Ms. Order said. "Imagine you're working on a project but can't find your notes or supplies. It's frustrating, right?"

Na'ima nodded, "I always lose my homework papers in my backpack."

"That's a common issue," Ms. Order acknowledged. "Here's what you can do. Use different folders or binders for each subject. Label them clearly so you know what goes where. This way, you can easily find what you need."

She handed out colorful folders and labels to each student. "Let's practice. Take out your materials and sort them into these folders."

As the students sorted their papers, Naudia exclaimed, "This makes everything so much easier to find!"

Organizing Space

Next, Ms. Order moved on to organizing space. "Now, let's talk about your study area. A cluttered desk can make it hard to concentrate."

Nyrie raised his hand, "My desk at home is always a mess. I can never find my pencils or books."

"Here's a tip," Ms. Order said. "Keep only what you need on your desk. Have designated areas for your supplies, like a cup for your pencils and a bookshelf. And remember to tidy up regularly."

She handed out small desk organizers and demonstrated how to arrange items. "Let's set up a sample desk together."

The students eagerly arranged their items, and soon, their desks were neat and orderly. Lenny looked pleased, "This feels so much better. I can see my workspace now!"

Practical Application

Ms. Order then gave each student a checklist. "Here's a checklist to help you stay organized. Use it daily to keep your materials and space in order."

The checklist included:

- Sort materials into folders
- Label folders and binders
- Keep desk tidy
- Return items to their designated places
- Minimize distractions

Reflection and Sharing

Ms. Order gathered the class for a reflection. "How do you feel about organizing your materials and space now?"

Noah smiled, "I feel more in control and less stressed."

Kimiyah added, "I think I'll be able to focus better on my homework."

"That's wonderful to hear," Ms. Order said. "Organization is a powerful skill that can help you in many ways. Keep practicing, and you'll see great improvements."

Conclusion

As the lesson ended, Ms. Order reminded her students, "Remember, staying organized takes practice, but it's worth the effort. A tidy space leads to a tidy mind, which can help you achieve your best in school and beyond."

The students left the classroom feeling empowered and ready to take on organizational challenges. They knew they could create a more orderly and productive environment at school and home with their new skills and tools.

Week 12: Enhancing Memory and Focus

Lesson 1: Memory Techniques

Lesson 1: Memory Techniques

Brainpower Boost in Learning Strategies

In the vibrant town of Memorization, Strategy Middle/High School was known for nurturing academic excellence and essential life skills. One of the most beloved teachers, Ms. Memory, the learning strategy teacher, was renowned for her ability to help students unlock the power of their minds.

One sunny morning, Ms. Memory, their enthusiastic instructor, was ready to unveil the secrets of enhancing memory and focus.

"Welcome to a day of brainpower boost!" Ms. Memory announced, her eyes sparkling with excitement. "Today, we're diving into memory techniques that'll make you recall information like a pro!"

Nyrie, the avid reader, was particularly intrigued. He often wished he could remember every detail of the captivating stories he devoured. "This sounds amazing, Ms. Memory!" he exclaimed.

Ms. Memory began by introducing mnemonic devices. She explained how creating vivid mental images and using acronyms could help link new information to existing knowledge, making it easier to retrieve later.

Ahlani, the history buff, was immediately drawn to the idea. She imagined using mnemonics to remember historical dates and events, turning her mind into a well-organized timeline.

Next, Ms. Memory introduced the concept of spaced repetition. She explained how reviewing information at specific intervals could solidify it in long-term memory.

Na'ima, the math enthusiast, found this particularly helpful. She realized how spaced repetition could revolutionize her study habits and ensure she effectively retained mathematical formulas and concepts.

Ms. Memory encouraged the students to try different techniques as the lesson progressed and discover what worked best. The budding inventor Noah found that combining visualization with spaced repetition helped him memorize complex scientific principles quickly.

By the end of the class, the students were buzzing with newfound confidence in their memory skills. They had unlocked a powerful tool that would aid them not only in their academic pursuits but also in their everyday lives.

Lesson 2:
Improving Concentration

Mind Masters: Sharpen Your Focus

In the focused town of Concentration, Strategy Middle/High School was a haven for students seeking to sharpen their minds and achieve their full potential. Mr. Concentrate, the esteemed learning strategy teacher, was known for his unique ability to guide students toward mastering the art of memory and focus.

One bright morning, Mr. Concentrate's classroom buzzed with anticipation. Today's lesson promised to be particularly exciting, as Mr. Concentrate was set to unveil the secrets of enhancing memory and focus.

"Welcome, scholars!" Mr. Concentrate's voice boomed with enthusiasm. "Today, we're embarking on a journey to unlock the incredible power of your minds! Get ready to learn techniques that will make you remember anything and stay focused like laser beams!"

Kimiyah, a determined learner who often struggled with staying on task, leaned forward in her seat, eager to absorb every word. Mason, a talented musician who usually felt overwhelmed by stage fright, hoped these techniques would help him stay calm and collected during performances.

Mr. Concentrate began by explaining the importance of focus. "Think of your mind as a powerful spotlight," he said. "When you focus, you direct that spotlight onto one specific thing, illuminating it with clarity. But distractions are like flickering shadows, pulling your attention away."

Levi, the tech-savvy student, nodded in understanding. He knew how easy it was to get sidetracked by notifications and online temptations.

Next, Mr. Concentrate introduced mindfulness techniques. He guided the students through a simple breathing exercise, encouraging them to focus on the present moment.

Nilan, the sports enthusiast, found this particularly helpful. He realized how mindfulness could improve his concentration during games, allowing him to make precise split-second decisions.

As the lesson progressed, Mr. Concentrate shared various memory-enhancing strategies. He emphasized the power of visualization, association, and repetition.

Naudia, the empathetic student, was fascinated by associating new information with familiar images or experiences. She saw how this could help her connect with the emotions and perspectives of others, enhancing her conflict-resolution skills.

By the end of the class, the students were brimming with excitement and newfound confidence. They had learned invaluable techniques to strengthen their memory and focus, which would undoubtedly empower them in their academic journeys and beyond. As they left the classroom, their minds were abuzz with possibilities, ready to tackle any challenge with unwavering concentration.

Week 13: Problem-Solving and Flexibility

Lesson 1: Steps to Effective Problem-Solving

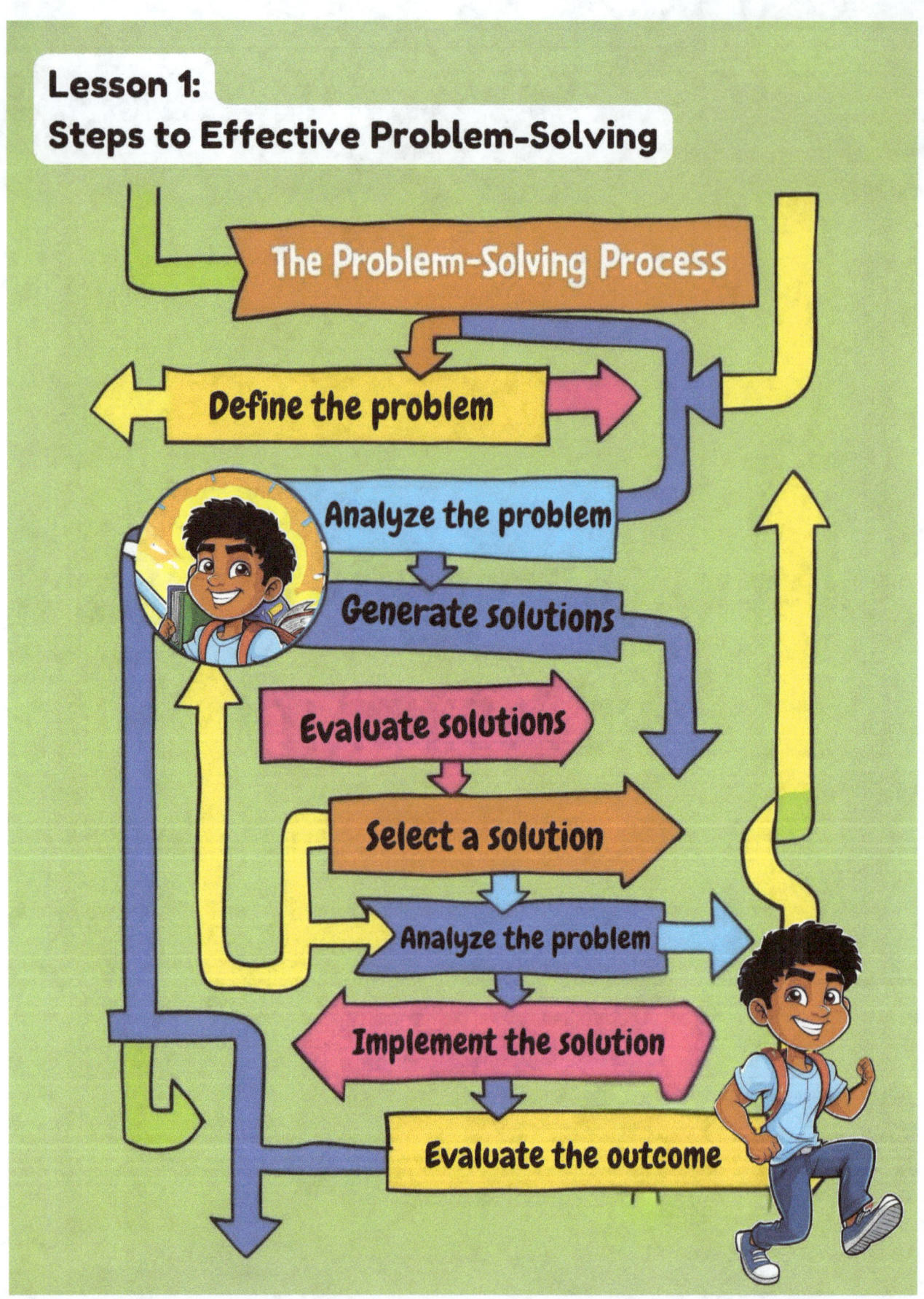

Lesson 1:
Steps to Effective Problem-Solving

From Flustered to Focused: Lenny's Problem-Solving Triumph

In the resourceful town of Eureka, nestled amidst rolling hills and bubbling streams, Strategy Middle/High School was a hub of innovation and creative thinking. Mr. Solver, the esteemed learning strategy teacher, was celebrated for his ability to guide students through the labyrinth of problems, transforming challenges into opportunities for growth.

One crisp autumn morning, Mr. Solver's classroom was abuzz with excitement. The day's lesson promised to equip the students with the essential steps to practical problem-solving.

"Welcome, problem-solvers!" Mr. Solver's voice resonated with enthusiasm. "Today, we're embarking on a quest to conquer any challenge that comes our way. Remember, every problem is an opportunity in disguise!"

Lenny, the science enthusiast who often felt overwhelmed by complex experiments, perked up. He was eager to learn strategies to help him navigate the intricacies of the scientific world. The social butterfly Nia also valued honing her problem-solving skills to improve her communication and time management.

Mr. Solver began by outlining the key steps:

1. **Identify the problem:** Clearly define the issue at hand.

2. **Gather information:** Collect relevant data and facts.

3. **Brainstorm solutions:** Generate various possible solutions, no matter how outlandish they may seem.

4. **Evaluate and choose:** Analyze each solution's pros and cons, then select the most promising one.

5. **Implement and review:** Put the chosen solution into action and assess its effectiveness.

As Mr. Solver elaborated on each step, the students eagerly participated, sharing their problem-solving experiences and offering creative suggestions. Lenny realized that his tendency to jump to conclusions often hindered his ability to identify the root cause of a problem. Nia recognized the importance of gathering diverse perspectives before settling on a solution.

By the end of the lesson, the students felt empowered. They had acquired a powerful toolkit that would enable them to tackle any problem with confidence and ingenuity. As they left the classroom, their minds were abuzz with ideas, ready to apply their newfound skills to their challenges.

Lesson 2: Developing Cognitive Flexibility

Lesson 2:
Developing Cognitive Flexibility

Hat Trick: Naudia's Journey to Understanding

In the adaptable town of Adaptability, Strategy Middle/High School was a haven for students seeking to cultivate mental agility and embrace change. Ms. Flex, the dynamic learning strategy teacher, was renowned for inspiring students to think outside the box and adapt to new situations with grace and resilience.

One sunny afternoon, Ms. Flex's classroom became a vibrant playground of ideas. The day's lesson focused on developing cognitive flexibility, shifting perspectives, and approaching problems from multiple angles.

"Welcome, flexible thinkers!" Ms. Flex's voice sparkled with enthusiasm. "Today, we're stretching our minds and embracing the beauty of change. Remember, the world is constantly evolving, and so should our thinking!"

Naudia, the empathetic student, was particularly captivated by the idea of cognitive flexibility. She saw how it could help her understand different viewpoints and navigate conflicts more easily. Noah, the budding inventor, also recognized the importance of adaptability in the creative process.

Ms. Flex introduced the concept of "thinking hats," a technique encouraging individuals to adopt different perspectives when analyzing a situation. She assigned each student a different colored hat, representing a specific thinking style:

- **White Hat:** Focus on facts and information.
- **Red Hat:** Express emotions and intuitions.
- **Black Hat:** Identify risks and weaknesses.
- **Yellow Hat:** Explore benefits and opportunities.
- **Green Hat:** Generate creative ideas and solutions.
- **Blue Hat:** Manage the thinking process and conclude.

The students eagerly donned their metaphorical hats and engaged in lively discussions, exploring a variety of scenarios from different angles. Naudia found that wearing the "red hat" helped her tap into her empathy and understand the emotional impact of a situation. Wearing the "green hat," Noah discovered a newfound ability to generate innovative solutions to complex problems.

By the end of the lesson, the students had embraced the power of cognitive flexibility. They had learned to appreciate the value of diverse perspectives and the importance of adapting their thinking to navigate the ever-changing world. As they left the classroom, their minds were brimming with possibilities, ready to embrace the challenges and opportunities ahead.

Week 14: Enhancing Self-Monitoring and Task Initiation

Lesson 1: Self-Monitoring Techniques

Lesson 1:
Self-Monitoring Techniques

Story Title: "Mirror, Mirror: Reflecting on Success in Self-Awarenessville"

In the reflective town of Self-Awarenessville, nestled amidst serene lakes and lush greenery, Strategy Middle/High School was a sanctuary for students seeking to cultivate self-awareness and personal growth. Mrs. Monitor, the insightful learning strategy teacher, was renowned for her ability to guide students in understanding their strengths, weaknesses, and progress.

One tranquil morning, Mrs. Monitor's classroom was bathed in soft sunlight. The day's lesson promised to illuminate the path to effective self-monitoring.

"Welcome, self-explorers!" Mrs. Monitor's voice resonated with warmth and encouragement. "Today, we're embarking on a journey of self-discovery. We'll learn to observe our thoughts, actions, and progress, empowering us to make positive changes and achieve our goals!"

Mason, the talented musician who often struggled with managing stress and anxiety, felt a sense of hope. He longed for tools to help him recognize his triggers and develop coping mechanisms. Naudia, the empathetic student, was also eager to enhance her self-monitoring skills better to understand her own emotions and those of others.

Mrs. Monitor began by explaining the importance of self-awareness. "Think of self-monitoring as a mirror reflecting your inner world," she said. "By observing your thoughts, feelings, and behaviors, you gain valuable insights into your strengths and areas for growth."

She then introduced various self-monitoring techniques, such as:

- **Thought tracking:** Keeping a journal to record thoughts and feelings.
- **Behavior checklists:** Creating checklists to monitor specific behaviors or habits.
- **Progress charts:** Tracking progress towards goals to visualize accomplishments and identify improvement areas.
- **Peer feedback:** Seeking constructive feedback from classmates to gain different perspectives.

As Mrs. Monitor elaborated on each technique, the students actively participated, sharing their experiences and challenges with self-monitoring. Mason realized that keeping a thought journal could help him identify patterns in his anxiety and develop strategies to manage it. Naudia recognized the value of peer feedback in understanding how her actions impacted others.

By the end of the lesson, the students felt empowered. They had acquired valuable tools to monitor their thoughts, actions, and progress, enabling them to make informed choices and strive for continuous improvement. As they left the classroom, they carried a newfound sense of self-awareness, ready to embark on their journey of personal growth.

Lesson 2:
Task Initiation Strategies

Ready, Set, Go! Overcoming Inertia in Procrastinationville

In the bustling town of Procrastinationville, where time seemed to slip through fingers like sand, Strategy Middle/High School was a beacon of hope for students struggling with task initiation. Mr. Initiate, the energetic learning strategy teacher, was celebrated for his ability to motivate students and help them overcome the inertia of procrastination.

One vibrant afternoon, Mr. Initiate's classroom was charged with a sense of purpose. The day's lesson focused on conquering procrastination and mastering the art of task initiation.

"Welcome, action-takers!" Mr. Initiate's voice crackled with energy. "Today, we're breaking free from procrastination and unleashing our full potential! Get ready to learn strategies that will propel you toward success!"

Kimiyah, the determined learner who often struggled with executive functioning skills, felt a surge of motivation. She yearned to overcome her tendency to delay tasks and embrace a proactive study approach.

Mr. Initiate began by addressing the root causes of procrastination. He explained how fear of failure, perfectionism, and lack of motivation could lead to delaying tasks.

He then introduced various task initiation strategies, such as:

- **Breaking down tasks:** Dividing large tasks into smaller, more manageable steps.
- **Setting SMART goals:** Creating specific, measurable, achievable, relevant, and time-bound goals.
- **Creating a schedule:** Developing a structured schedule to allocate time for different tasks.
- **Eliminating distractions:** Minimizing distractions and creating a conducive work environment.
- **Rewarding progress:** Celebrating accomplishments to maintain motivation.

As Mr. Initiate elaborated on each strategy, the students actively participated, sharing their experiences with procrastination and brainstorming ways to overcome it. Kimiyah realized that breaking down her assignments into smaller steps would make them feel less daunting and more achievable.

By the end of the lesson, the students were buzzing with newfound energy and determination. They had learned valuable strategies to overcome procrastination and take charge of their tasks. As they left the classroom, they felt empowered, ready to tackle their goals with renewed vigor and a proactive mindset.

Week 15: Integrating Executive Functioning with Academics

Lesson 1:
Executive Functioning in Daily Learning

Lesson 1:
Executive Functioning in Daily Learning

Brain Power Unleashed: Executive Functioning in Actionville

In the bustling town of Actionville, where productivity and efficiency reigned supreme, Strategy Middle/High School was a haven for students seeking to harness the power of their executive functions. Mrs. Executive, the esteemed learning strategy teacher, was renowned for her ability to guide students in mastering the skills of planning, organizing, and self-regulating their learning.

One dynamic morning, Mrs. Executive's classroom was abuzz with energy. The day's lesson promised to unlock the secrets of applying executive functioning skills to everyday learning.

"Welcome, executive masterminds!" Mrs. Executive's voice crackled with enthusiasm. "Today, we're diving deep into the world of executive functions and discovering how they can supercharge your learning! Get ready to unleash your brain power!"

Kimiyah, the determined learner who often struggled with executive functioning skills, leaned forward in her seat, her eyes gleaming with anticipation. She yearned to learn strategies to help her organize her thoughts, manage her time effectively, and achieve her academic goals.

Mrs. Executive began by explaining the core executive functions:

- **Working memory:** The ability to hold and manipulate information in your mind.
- **Inhibitory control:** The ability to resist distractions and impulses.
- **Cognitive flexibility:** The ability to shift perspectives and adapt to new situations.

She then demonstrated how these skills play a crucial role in everyday learning tasks, such as:

- **Planning and prioritizing:** Breaking down assignments, setting deadlines, and creating a study schedule.
- **Organizing materials:** Keeping notebooks, binders, and digital files tidy and accessible.
- **Managing time:** Estimating task duration, avoiding procrastination, and staying on track.

- **Self-monitoring:** Checking work for accuracy, reflecting on progress, and seeking help when needed.

As Mrs. Executive elaborated on each skill, the students eagerly participated, sharing their experiences and challenges with executive functioning. Kimiyah realized her tendency to procrastinate stemmed from a lack of planning and organization.

By the end of the lesson, the students were buzzing with newfound understanding. They had gained valuable insights into the power of executive functions and how to apply them to their daily learning. As they left the classroom, they carried a sense of empowerment, ready to tackle their academic challenges with a strategic and organized approach.

Lesson 2:
Reflection and Goal Adjustment

Charting Your Course: Navigating Success in Reflectionville

In the reflective town of Reflectionville, where growth and self-improvement were cherished values, Strategy Middle/High School was a haven for students seeking to refine their learning strategies and achieve their full potential. Mr. Adjust, the wise learning strategy teacher, was celebrated for his ability to guide students in reflecting on their progress and making necessary adjustments to reach their goals.

One peaceful afternoon, Mr. Adjust's classroom was filled with introspection. The lesson focused on the importance of reflection and goal adjustment in learning.

"Welcome, reflective learners!" Mr. Adjust's voice exuded calmness and wisdom. "Today, we're taking a step back to examine our journey. Remember, the path to success is not always linear, and it's essential to adapt and refine our strategies along the way."

Levi, the tech-savvy student, was particularly intrigued. He understood the value of iterative processes in software development and was curious to see how this applied to his learning.

Mr. Adjust began by emphasizing the importance of self-assessment. "Reflection is like a compass guiding you towards your destination," he explained. "By honestly evaluating your progress, you can identify your strengths, weaknesses, and areas for improvement."

He then introduced various reflection techniques, such as:

- **Journaling:** Writing down thoughts, feelings, and observations about the learning process.
- **Self-questioning:** Asking oneself probing questions to gain deeper insights.
- **Peer feedback:** Seeking constructive criticism from classmates to gain different perspectives.
- **Progress tracking:** Reviewing completed work and comparing it to initial goals.

As Mr. Adjust elaborated on each technique, the students actively participated, sharing their experiences with reflection and goal setting. Levi realized that he often focused solely on the result, neglecting to appreciate the learning that occurred along the way.

By the end of the lesson, the students had embraced the power of reflection and goal adjustment. They understood that setbacks and challenges were natural parts of the learning process and that adapting their strategies was vital to success. As they left the classroom, they carried a renewed sense of purpose, ready to navigate their learning journeys with confidence and resilience.

Unit 4:

The Superpower of Good Habits
(Weeks 16-21)

Week 16: Understanding Habits

Introduction to Unit 4

Imagine having a superpower that could effortlessly guide you towards your goals, even when motivation dwindles. That superpower exists, and it's called the power of good habits! They are the subtle, everyday actions that shape our lives and unlock our true potential. Consider the simple acts of brushing your teeth or tying your shoelaces—you do these things automatically without much thought. Now envision applying that same automatic power to studying, staying organized, managing your time, or even coping with stress. This is the magic we're going to uncover in this unit.

We'll delve into the fascinating science behind habit formation, explore how to break free from those pesky bad habits that hold us back, and most importantly, learn how to cultivate new habits that align with our aspirations and dreams. Just like superheroes train their powers, we need to practice and nurture our good habits. It requires effort, but I assure you, the rewards are extraordinary. Once you harness the power of good habits, there's no limit to what you can achieve!

Lesson 1: The Science of Habits

Lesson 1: Understanding the Habit Loop - The Key to Transformation

Naudia's Quest for Inner Peace

Naudia, known for her warm heart and friendly nature, found herself entangled in an unusual predicament. Lately, she'd been getting into disagreements more frequently than ever before. It seemed like the slightest inconvenience triggered an outburst, leaving her feeling frustrated and confused. She noticed a pattern; whenever schoolwork piled up or stress mounted, she'd snap at her friends and family, her patience wearing thin.

Determined to address this issue, Naudia confided in her teacher, Ms. Harmony. Ms. Harmony, with a gentle smile, introduced Naudia to the concept of the habit loop: a cycle consisting of a trigger, a behavior, and a reward. She explained that understanding this cycle is crucial to transforming any habit. Together, they embarked on a journey of self-discovery. Ms. Harmony helped Naudia recognize that stress acted as her trigger, snapping at others was her impulsive behavior, and the brief sense of relief she experienced after venting served as her reward.

Armed with this newfound knowledge, Naudia began to observe her own behavior more closely. She noticed how stress often manifested physically—tight shoulders, a racing heart. Whenever she recognized these signs, she'd consciously take a deep breath, breaking the cycle before it escalated. She replaced her impulsive reactions with mindful responses, choosing to communicate her feelings calmly and assertively. Gradually, Naudia noticed a transformation. Her relationships improved, and she felt a sense of control returning to her life.

Lesson 2: Building New Habits - Laying the Foundation for Success

Na'ima's Math Magic

Na'ima, a math enthusiast, always found herself struggling with maintaining a consistent study routine. She'd often procrastinate until the last minute, leading to a whirlwind of stress and anxiety. Despite her love for the subject, her grades didn't reflect her true potential.

Seeking guidance, Na'ima approached her teacher, Ms. Consistency. Ms. Consistency, recognizing Na'ima's predicament, introduced her to a powerful technique known as "habit stacking." This involved linking a new habit to an existing one, leveraging the existing routine to pave the way for the new behavior. Intrigued, Na'ima decided to give it a try. She chose to stack her new habit of studying math for 30 minutes each day onto her existing habit of brushing her teeth after dinner.

At first, it felt a bit awkward. The transition from brushing her teeth to opening her math textbook felt forced. But Na'ima persevered. She placed her math books on her desk, ready and waiting. As days turned into weeks, she noticed a remarkable shift. The once-forced transition became smoother, and soon, studying math after brushing her teeth felt as natural as the brushing itself. Her grades improved, and more importantly, she felt a sense of accomplishment and control over her studies.

Week 17: Building Positive Habits

Lesson 1: Establishing New Habits

Lesson 1:
Establishing New Habits

Ahlani's History Hustle

Ahlani loved history. Ancient civilizations, historical figures, important dates – she devoured it all. But her passion for the past sometimes clashed with her present-day struggles with organization. Her notes were scattered, her backpack a black hole, and her study schedule nonexistent. This often left Ahlani feeling overwhelmed and frustrated, especially when it came time to prepare for tests.

One day, in their learning strategies class with Mr. Orderly, they discussed the power of habits. Mr. Orderly explained how small, consistent actions could lead to big changes. He introduced the idea of "habit cues" – linking a new habit to an existing one. Ahlani's eyes lit up. She realized she could use her love for history as a cue! Every time she sat down to watch her favorite historical documentary, she would first spend 15 minutes organizing her history notes and planning her study time for the week.

At first, it felt a bit forced. Ahlani was eager to dive into the documentary. But she stuck with it. She placed her history binder and planner next to the TV as a visual reminder. Gradually, the transition became smoother. Organizing her notes before her historical TV time became as natural as grabbing the remote. Ahlani felt a sense of calm replace her usual pre-test panic. Her grades even started to improve as she consistently reviewed and organized her material.

Lesson 2: Habit Tracking and Reflection

Lesson 2:
Habit Tracking and Reflection

Nilan's Game Plan

Nilan was a star athlete, excelling in every sport he tried. But his natural talent often masked his struggles with planning and organization. He'd forget practice times, misplace equipment, and leave homework assignments until the last minute. This chaotic approach started to affect both his athletic performance and his grades.

In their learning strategies class with Ms. Strategize, they explored the importance of habit tracking and reflection. Ms. Strategize introduced the class to different tracking methods, from simple checklists to colorful habit trackers. Nilan, inspired by the idea of leveling up his organizational skills like he leveled up in his video games, decided to create a habit tracker for his athletic and academic goals.

He used different colors for different habits – green for completing homework, blue for attending practices, and red for remembering his equipment. Each day, he'd mark his progress with a satisfying checkmark. At the end of each week, Nilan would take a few minutes to reflect on his tracker. He noticed patterns – he was consistently good at attending practices but often forgot his equipment on Mondays. This awareness allowed him to adjust his routine, packing his bag the night before.

Nilan discovered that tracking his habits not only helped him stay organized but also motivated him to keep going. Seeing those checkmarks accumulate gave him a sense of accomplishment and fueled his determination to improve.

Week 18: Replacing Negative Habits

Introduction to Week 18

This week, we're turning our attention to those pesky negative habits that might be holding us back from reaching our full potential. Just like superheroes confront villains, we need to face those habits that don't serve us well. But instead of fighting them head-on, we'll learn how to outsmart them with clever strategies and replace them with positive habits that empower us. Remember, breaking free from negative habits is a journey, not a battle. It takes time, patience, and self-compassion. So let's embark on this adventure together, armed with knowledge and a determination to transform those habits into stepping stones towards success!

Lesson 1: Identifying Triggers and Patterns

Lesson 1:
Identifying Triggers and Patterns

Lenny's Lab Breakthrough

Lenny loved science, but complex experiments often left him feeling overwhelmed. He had a habit of procrastinating, leaving projects until the last minute, which only amplified his anxiety and sometimes led to mistakes in the lab.

In their learning strategies class with Ms. Analyze, they discussed the importance of identifying triggers and patterns in negative habits. Ms. Analyze explained how recognizing the cues that precede a negative habit can help us interrupt the cycle and make different choices. Lenny realized that his trigger was the feeling of intimidation when faced with a challenging experiment. This feeling would lead him to avoid the task, resulting in procrastination and increased stress.

Armed with this awareness, Lenny started to pay closer attention to his thoughts and feelings when a new experiment was introduced. He noticed the familiar tightness in his chest and the negative self-talk creeping in. But this time, instead of giving in, he took a deep breath and reminded himself of past successes. He broke down the experiment into smaller, more manageable steps, focusing on one task at a time. This approach helped him overcome his initial fear and tackle the project with more confidence and less procrastination.

Lesson 2: Strategies for Change

Mason's Melody of Calm

Mason, a talented musician, often struggled with performance anxiety. He had a habit of negative self-talk before auditions or concerts, which would escalate his stress and sometimes affect his performance.

In their learning strategies class with Mr. Positive, they explored different strategies for changing negative habits. Mr. Positive emphasized the importance of replacing negative thoughts with positive affirmations and developing coping mechanisms to manage stress. Mason decided to try a combination of these strategies.

He started by creating a list of positive affirmations, focusing on his strengths and past successes. He would repeat these affirmations to himself whenever he felt anxiety creeping in. He also learned relaxation techniques like deep breathing and progressive muscle relaxation to calm his nerves before performances.

At first, it felt a bit awkward to counter his usual negative thoughts with positive ones. But with practice, it became easier. Mason even incorporated his love for music into his coping strategy, creating a playlist of calming melodies to listen to before performances. Gradually, he noticed a shift in his mindset. He felt more confident and in control, and his performances became more enjoyable and less stressful.

Week 19: Developing Consistency

Introduction to Week 19

Imagine planting a seed. You nurture it with water and sunlight, but it doesn't sprout overnight. It takes time, consistent care, and patience for it to grow into a strong plant. Developing good habits is similar. It's not about sudden bursts of effort but about steady, consistent action over time. This week, we'll explore the incredible power of consistency and learn practical strategies to cultivate this essential skill. Just like a gardener tends to their plants, we'll learn to nurture our habits, day after day, until they become an integral part of who we are.

Lesson 1:
The Power of Consistency

Kimiyah's Consistent Climb

Kimiyah was a determined learner, but she often felt overwhelmed by the demands of school. She had a habit of starting strong with new projects or study routines, but her enthusiasm would often fade after a few days, leaving her feeling discouraged.

In their learning strategies class with Mr. Steady, they discussed the power of consistency. Mr. Steady explained how consistent effort, even in small increments, could lead to significant progress over time. He shared the analogy of a snowball rolling down a hill, gaining momentum and size with each rotation. Kimiyah realized that her lack of consistency was hindering her progress, like a snowball that kept melting before it could gather momentum.

Inspired by this analogy, Kimiyah decided to apply the principle of consistency to her study habits. She started by setting realistic goals, committing to just 30 minutes of focused study each day. She also created a visual reminder of her "snowball effect," drawing a small snowball gradually growing larger as it rolled down a hill. Whenever she felt her motivation waning, she would look at her drawing and remind herself that consistent effort, even in small amounts, would eventually lead to a significant accumulation of knowledge and skills.

Lesson 2: Strategies for Maintaining Consistency

Lesson 2:
Strategies for Maintaining Consistency

Nyrie's Creative Calm

Nyrie, a talented artist, often struggled with staying calm and managing stress. He had a habit of getting easily frustrated when things didn't go as planned, which would disrupt his creative flow and sometimes lead to him abandoning projects altogether.

In their learning strategies class with Ms. Tranquility, they explored strategies for maintaining consistency, even when faced with challenges. Ms. Tranquility emphasized the importance of self-care, mindfulness, and breaking down tasks into smaller, more manageable steps. Nyrie decided to incorporate these strategies into his artistic process.

He started by creating a dedicated workspace where he could focus without distractions. He also incorporated mindfulness practices, like taking short breaks to stretch or practice deep breathing, whenever he felt frustration building up. He learned to break down his larger art projects into smaller, more achievable tasks, celebrating each milestone along the way.

These changes helped Nyrie maintain a more consistent creative flow. He felt calmer and more in control, even when facing setbacks. He learned to embrace the process, appreciating the small steps that contributed to the larger picture. His artistic confidence grew as he experienced the satisfaction of completing projects and expressing himself through his art.

Week 20: Habitual Growth and Adaptation

Introduction to Week 20

Congratulations! You've journeyed through the exciting world of habits, from understanding the habit loop to establishing new routines and overcoming obstacles. This week, we celebrate your progress and explore the ongoing nature of habit development. Just like we grow and change, our habits need to adapt and evolve with us. We'll learn how to fine-tune our habits to support our personal growth and reflect on the incredible transformations we've experienced on this journey.

Lesson 1: Adapting Habits for Growth

Lesson 1:
Adapting Habits for Growth

Nia's Time-Traveling Transformation

Nia, a social butterfly with a knack for communication, often struggled with time management. She loved being involved in everything, but her packed schedule sometimes left her feeling overwhelmed and scattered.

In their learning strategies class with Mr. Evolve, they discussed the importance of adapting habits for growth. Mr. Evolve explained how our habits should be flexible and responsive to our changing needs and goals. He encouraged the class to view habits as tools that can be adjusted and refined to support their personal development.

Nia realized that her time management habits needed a makeover. She loved her social commitments, but she also wanted to prioritize her academic goals and personal well-being. She started by revisiting her schedule, identifying her priorities, and allocating time blocks for different activities. She also learned to say "no" to some commitments, recognizing that it's okay to set boundaries to protect her time and energy.

As Nia adapted her habits, she discovered a newfound sense of balance. She was still able to enjoy her social life, but she also had dedicated time for focused study and self-care. She felt more organized and in control, and her academic performance improved as she learned to prioritize and manage her time effectively.

Lesson 2: Reflecting on Habitual Progress

Lesson 2:
Reflecting on Habitual Progress

Noah's Organized Oasis

Noah, a budding inventor with a knack for creativity, often struggled with focus and organization. His workspace was a whirlwind of ideas and inventions, but this chaotic environment sometimes hindered his progress.

In their learning strategies class with Ms. Reflect, they discussed the importance of reflecting on habitual progress. Ms. Reflect encouraged the class to celebrate their achievements, acknowledge their challenges, and learn from their experiences.

Noah realized that while he had made progress in developing organizational habits, he still had room for improvement. He took some time to review his journey, acknowledging the positive changes he had made, such as creating a designated workspace and implementing a daily cleanup routine. He also recognized areas where he could continue to grow, such as managing distractions and prioritizing tasks.

Inspired by his reflections, Noah decided to implement a weekly "organization check-in" where he would assess his progress, identify any challenges, and adjust his strategies as needed. This regular reflection helped him stay on track and maintain his organizational habits, creating a more conducive environment for his inventive spirit to flourish.

Week 21: Integrating Good Habits with Academics

Introduction to Week 21

We've explored the incredible power of habits and how they can transform our lives. This week, we'll focus on integrating these powerful tools into our academic journey. Just as a skilled craftsman uses the right tools for the job, we'll learn how to apply good habits to enhance our learning, boost our productivity, and achieve our academic goals. Get ready to unlock your full academic potential by harnessing the power of good habits!

Lesson 1: Good Habits in Daily Learning

Lesson 1:
Good Habits in Daily Learning

Levi's Problem-Solving Power-Up

Levi, a tech-savvy student with a passion for problem-solving, often found himself getting stuck on challenging assignments. He had a habit of jumping right into problems without a clear plan, which sometimes led to frustration and wasted time.

In their learning strategies class with Ms. Apply, they discussed the importance of integrating good habits into daily learning. Ms. Apply emphasized the power of planning, organization, and self-reflection in tackling academic challenges.

Levi realized that his approach to problem-solving needed a more structured approach. He started by incorporating planning into his routine, breaking down complex problems into smaller, more manageable steps. He also began using visual organizers and mind maps to clarify his thoughts and identify different solution paths. He even started a "problem-solving journal" where he would reflect on his process, noting what worked well and what could be improved.

These new habits transformed Levi's approach to learning. He felt more confident and focused when tackling challenging assignments. He learned to embrace mistakes as learning opportunities and developed a growth mindset that fueled his academic progress.

Lesson 2: Reflection and Goal Adjustment

Lesson 2:
Reflection and Goal Adjustment

Kenlyn's Fluent Flow

Kenlyn, a peacemaker with a desire to improve her reading fluency, often felt self-conscious when reading aloud in class. She had a habit of stumbling over words and losing her place, which made her feel anxious and discouraged.

In their learning strategies class with Mr. Adapt, they discussed the importance of reflection and goal adjustment in the learning process. Mr. Adapt emphasized that learning is a journey, not a destination, and that setbacks and challenges are opportunities for growth.

Kenlyn realized that her goal of improving reading fluency required ongoing effort and adaptation. She started by setting smaller, more achievable goals, such as practicing reading aloud for 15 minutes each day. She also incorporated strategies like pre-reading and breaking down longer texts into smaller chunks. She even started recording herself reading aloud to track her progress and identify areas for improvement.

Through consistent practice and reflection, Kenlyn gradually gained confidence and fluency. She learned to embrace mistakes as part of the learning process and celebrated her progress along the way. She even started volunteering to read aloud in class, sharing her newfound fluency with her peers.

Unit 5:

Superpowers to Academics

Introduction to Unit 5

Get ready to unleash your inner academic superhero! Throughout this unit, we'll explore how the superpowers we've developed—mindfulness, executive functioning skills, and positive habits—can be applied to specific academic areas. We'll dive into reading strategies, writing techniques, math problem-solving, and effective study skills, discovering how our newfound powers can transform our learning experience. Just as superheroes use their unique abilities to overcome challenges and achieve extraordinary feats, we'll learn to harness our strengths to conquer academic obstacles and unlock our full potential.

Week 22:
Reading Strategies

Introduction to Week 22

Reading is a superpower in itself! It opens doors to new worlds, expands our knowledge, and sparks our imagination. This week, we'll explore essential reading strategies that can help us become more confident and effective readers. From decoding and phonics skills to comprehension and fluency, we'll discover how to unlock the magic of words and make reading an enjoyable and rewarding adventure.

**Lesson 1:
Decoding and Phonics Skills**

Lesson 1:
Decoding and Phonics Skills

Nyrie's Decoding Discovery

Nyrie, an avid reader who sometimes struggled with decoding unfamiliar words, often felt his reading flow interrupted by these stumbling blocks. He loved getting lost in stories, but the struggle to decipher words sometimes made it difficult to fully immerse himself in the narrative.

In their learning strategies class with Mr. Wordsmith, they discussed the importance of decoding and phonics skills as the foundation for fluent reading. Mr. Wordsmith explained how breaking down words into smaller units of sound could unlock their pronunciation and meaning.

Nyrie, intrigued by this concept, started paying closer attention to the sounds and patterns within words. He practiced breaking down words into syllables and identifying common phonics rules. He even created flashcards with challenging words, using different colors to represent different sounds.

As Nyrie's decoding skills improved, he noticed a significant difference in his reading fluency. He could navigate unfamiliar words with more confidence, and his reading became smoother and more enjoyable. He felt a sense of accomplishment as he unlocked the code of language, opening up a world of literary adventures.

Lesson 2:
Comprehension and Fluency

Na'ima's Mathematical Reading Adventure

Na'ima, a math lover, often approached reading with a focus on facts and figures. She enjoyed informational texts and solving word problems, but she sometimes struggled to connect with stories and understand the nuances of character emotions and plot development.

In their learning strategies class with Ms. Bookworm, they discussed the importance of comprehension and fluency in unlocking the full meaning of a text. Ms. Bookworm explained how active reading strategies, such as visualizing, predicting, and connecting with the text, could enhance understanding and enjoyment.

Na'ima, eager to improve her comprehension skills, started experimenting with these strategies. She began visualizing the scenes and characters as she read, bringing the stories to life in her imagination. She also started making predictions about what might happen next, engaging with the text in a more interactive way.

As Na'ima practiced these strategies, she discovered a newfound appreciation for stories. She began to connect with the characters, understand their motivations, and appreciate the author's craft. Her reading fluency also improved as she became more engaged and immersed in the narratives.

Week 23: Reading Strategies Continued

Introduction to Week 23

Last week, we embarked on our reading adventure, exploring decoding and comprehension skills. This week, we'll delve deeper into strategies that can elevate our reading to new heights. We'll discover how to unlock the power of words through vocabulary building and explore techniques for reading with deeper understanding and purpose. Get ready to expand your reading horizons and become a true word wizard!

Lesson 1: Vocabulary Building

Lesson 1: Vocabulary Building

Ahlani's Historical Vocabulary Quest

Ahlani, a history enthusiast, often encountered unfamiliar words and terms in her readings. While she loved learning about the past, these vocabulary hurdles sometimes hindered her comprehension and made her feel less confident in her historical knowledge.

In their learning strategies class with Ms. Lexicon, they discussed the importance of vocabulary building as a key to unlocking deeper understanding and appreciation of any subject. Ms. Lexicon explained how expanding their word knowledge could open doors to new ideas and perspectives.

Ahlani, eager to enhance her historical vocabulary, started incorporating new strategies into her reading routine. She began keeping a vocabulary journal, jotting down unfamiliar words and their definitions. She also used context clues to decipher the meaning of words within the text. She even started playing word games and puzzles to make vocabulary building more engaging and fun.

As Ahlani's vocabulary grew, she noticed a significant improvement in her reading comprehension and her overall understanding of historical concepts. She felt more confident discussing historical events and expressing her ideas with precision and clarity.

Lesson 2: Reading for Understanding

Lenny's Scientific Reading Breakthrough

Lenny, a science enthusiast, often felt overwhelmed by the dense information in his science textbooks. He had a habit of passively reading through the material, which sometimes led to confusion and difficulty retaining the key concepts.

In their learning strategies class with Ms. Insight, they discussed the importance of active reading strategies for deeper understanding. Ms. Insight explained how techniques like annotating, summarizing, and questioning the text could enhance comprehension and retention.

Lenny, eager to improve his scientific reading skills, started experimenting with these strategies. He began annotating his textbook, highlighting key terms, jotting down questions in the margins, and summarizing important concepts in his own words. He also started using graphic organizers to visualize complex processes and relationships.

As Lenny practiced these active reading strategies, he noticed a significant improvement in his understanding and retention of scientific information. He felt more engaged with the material and could connect concepts more easily. He even started enjoying his science readings more as he actively participated in the learning process.

Week 24: Math Strategies

Introduction to Week 24

Math is more than just numbers and equations; it's a powerful tool for understanding the world around us. This week, we'll explore how our superpowers can help us unlock the magic of math. We'll delve into problem-solving techniques, discover the real-life applications of mathematical concepts, and learn to approach math with confidence and curiosity. Get ready to transform into math masters!

Lesson 1: Problem-Solving Techniques

$5y - 3 = 2y + 12$
STEP 1: SUBTRACT 2Y2Y2Y FROM BOTH SIDES:
$5y - 2y - 3 = 125y - 2y - 3 = 125y - 2y - 3 = 12$
$3y - 3 = 123y - 3 = 123y - 3 = 12$
STEP 2: ADD 3 TO BOTH SIDES:
$3y = 153y = 153y = 15$
STEP 3: DIVIDE BY 3:
$y = 5y = 5y = 5$

WORKING MATH PROBLEM

$3x + 5 = 2x + 11$
STEP 1: SUBTRACT 2X2X2X FROM BOTH SIDES:
$3x - 2x + 5 = 113x - 2x + 5 = 113x - 2x + 5 = 11$
$x + 5 = 11x + 5 = 11x + 5 = 11$
STEP 2: SUBTRACT 5 FROM BOTH SIDES:
$x = 6x = 6x = 6$

Lesson 1: Problem-Solving Techniques

Noah's Inventive Problem-Solving

Noah, a budding inventor, loved tinkering with gadgets and creating new contraptions. But when it came to solving math problems, he often felt lost and overwhelmed. He had a habit of rushing through problems, making careless mistakes, and giving up easily when faced with challenges.

In their learning strategies class with Mr. Solve, they discussed the importance of applying problem-solving techniques to approach math challenges strategically. Mr. Solve emphasized the power of breaking down problems, visualizing solutions, and persevering through setbacks.

Noah, eager to improve his math skills, started incorporating these techniques into his approach. He began by carefully reading and understanding the problem before jumping into calculations. He used diagrams and visual aids to represent the problem and explore different solution paths. He also learned to embrace mistakes as learning opportunities, analyzing his errors to deepen his understanding.

As Noah practiced these problem-solving techniques, he noticed a significant improvement in his math performance. He felt more confident and capable when tackling challenging problems. He learned to approach math with a growth mindset, viewing mistakes as stepping stones towards mastery.

Lesson 2:
Real-Life Application

Lesson 2: Real-Life Application

Na'ima's Budgeting Breakthrough

Na'ima, a math lover, enjoyed the challenge of solving equations and manipulating numbers. However, she sometimes struggled to see the relevance of math in her everyday life.

In their learning strategies class with Ms. Real-World, they explored the real-life applications of math concepts. Ms. Real-World showed how math is used in various contexts, from budgeting and shopping to cooking and building.

Na'ima, intrigued by this perspective, started noticing math everywhere she looked. She began applying her math skills to real-life situations, such as calculating discounts at the store, budgeting her allowance, and even measuring ingredients for her favorite recipes.

As Na'ima experienced the practical applications of math, she developed a deeper appreciation for its relevance and power. She realized that math wasn't just an abstract subject confined to textbooks; it was a tool that could help her navigate and understand the world around her.

Week 25: Math Strategies Continued

Introduction to Week 25

We're continuing our exploration of math strategies this week, focusing on how to deepen our understanding and expand our problem-solving toolbox. We'll discover techniques for enhancing our mathematical thinking and explore the vast array of tools and resources available to support our mathematical journey. Get ready to level up your math skills!

Lesson 1:
Enhancing Mathematical Understanding

Use <, >, or = to compare the fractions.

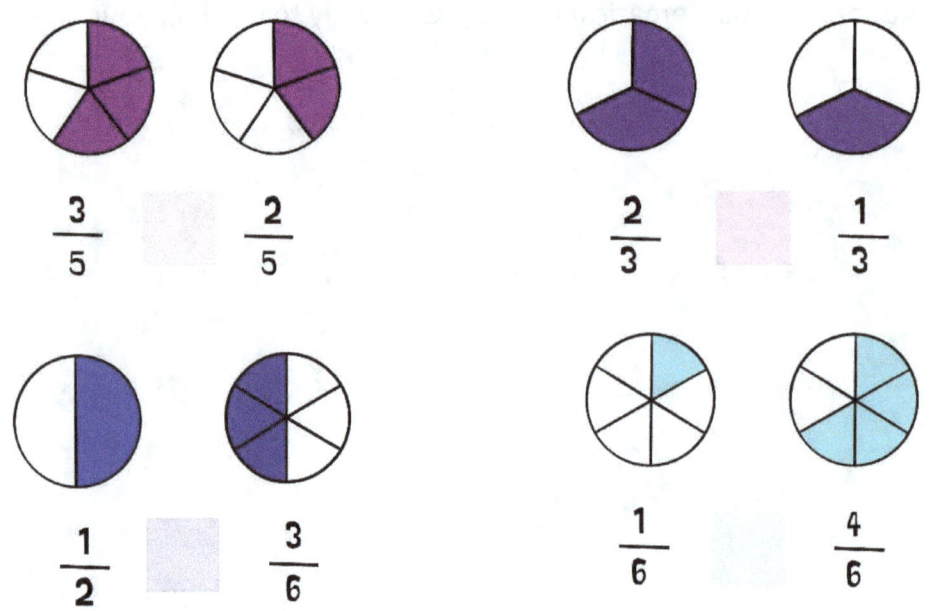

Write fraction of the colored part in each circle. Then, compare using >, <, or =.

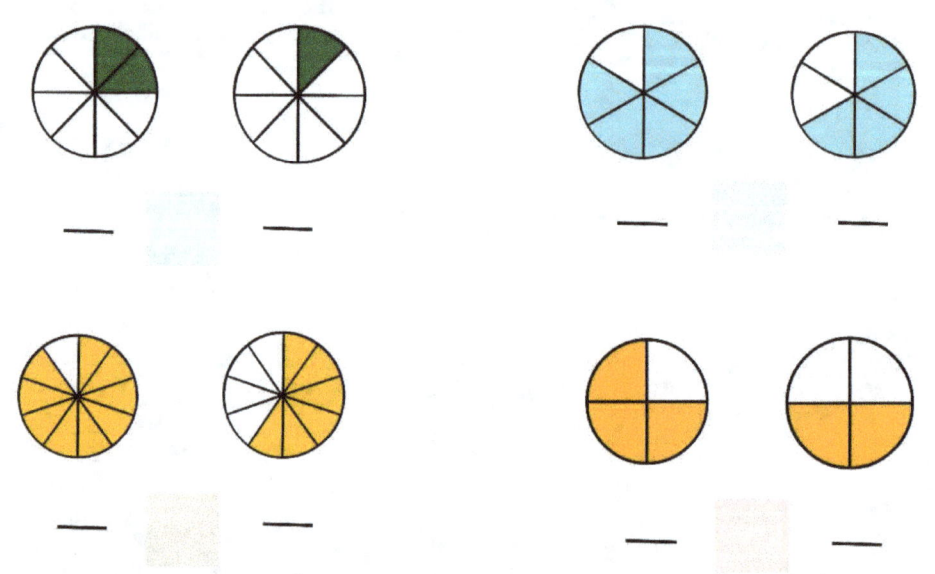

Lesson 1:
Enhancing Mathematical Understanding

Kimiyah's Conceptual Connections

Kimiyah, a determined learner, approached math with a focus on memorizing formulas and procedures. While she could often solve problems correctly, she sometimes struggled to grasp the underlying concepts and connect different mathematical ideas.

In their learning strategies class with Mr. Concept, they discussed the importance of developing conceptual understanding in math. Mr. Concept explained how understanding the "why" behind mathematical principles could deepen their learning and make problem-solving more intuitive.

Kimiyah, eager to enhance her mathematical understanding, started incorporating new strategies into her practice. She began asking "why" questions, exploring the reasoning behind formulas and procedures. She also started making connections between different mathematical concepts, looking for patterns and relationships. She even started creating her own visual representations and examples to illustrate mathematical ideas.

As Kimiyah focused on conceptual understanding, she noticed a shift in her approach to math. She felt more confident and capable when tackling new challenges. She could apply her knowledge more flexibly and solve problems with greater insight and creativity.

Lesson 2: Using Math Tools and Resources

Levi's Digital Math Discovery

Levi, a tech-savvy student, enjoyed using technology for learning and entertainment. However, he hadn't explored the vast array of digital tools and resources available to support his math learning.

In their learning strategies class with Ms. Tech, they discussed the benefits of utilizing math tools and resources. Ms. Tech introduced them to various online platforms, interactive simulations, and educational apps that could enhance their understanding and engagement with math.

Levi, excited by these possibilities, started exploring different math tools and resources. He discovered interactive simulations that allowed him to visualize mathematical concepts in action. He found online platforms with practice problems and tutorials tailored to his specific needs. He even started using educational math games to make learning more fun and engaging.

As Levi incorporated these tools and resources into his math practice, he noticed a significant improvement in his understanding and confidence. He could visualize abstract concepts, practice skills in a personalized way, and access support whenever he needed it. He realized that technology could be a powerful ally in his mathematical journey.

Week 26:
Science Strategies

Introduction to Week 26

Science is all about exploring the wonders of the world around us, from the smallest atoms to the vastness of space. This week, we'll discover how our superpowers can help us become more effective scientists. We'll delve into the power of hands-on learning, explore how to connect scientific concepts, and learn to approach science with curiosity, creativity, and a thirst for discovery. Get ready to unleash your inner scientist!

Lesson 1: Hands-On Learning

Lesson 1:
Hands-On Learning

Lenny's Electrifying Experiment

Lenny, a science enthusiast, loved reading about scientific discoveries and theories. However, he sometimes struggled to grasp complex concepts until he could see them in action.

In their learning strategies class with Ms. Experiment, they discussed the importance of hands-on learning in science. Ms. Experiment explained how engaging with scientific principles through experiments and activities could deepen their understanding and spark their curiosity.

Lenny, eager to experience science firsthand, started incorporating hands-on activities into his learning. He conducted experiments at home, built models to illustrate scientific concepts, and even started a small garden to observe plant growth and development.

As Lenny engaged in hands-on learning, he noticed a significant improvement in his grasp of scientific concepts. He could visualize abstract ideas, connect theories to real-world phenomena, and develop a deeper appreciation for the scientific process.

Lesson 2: Concept Mapping

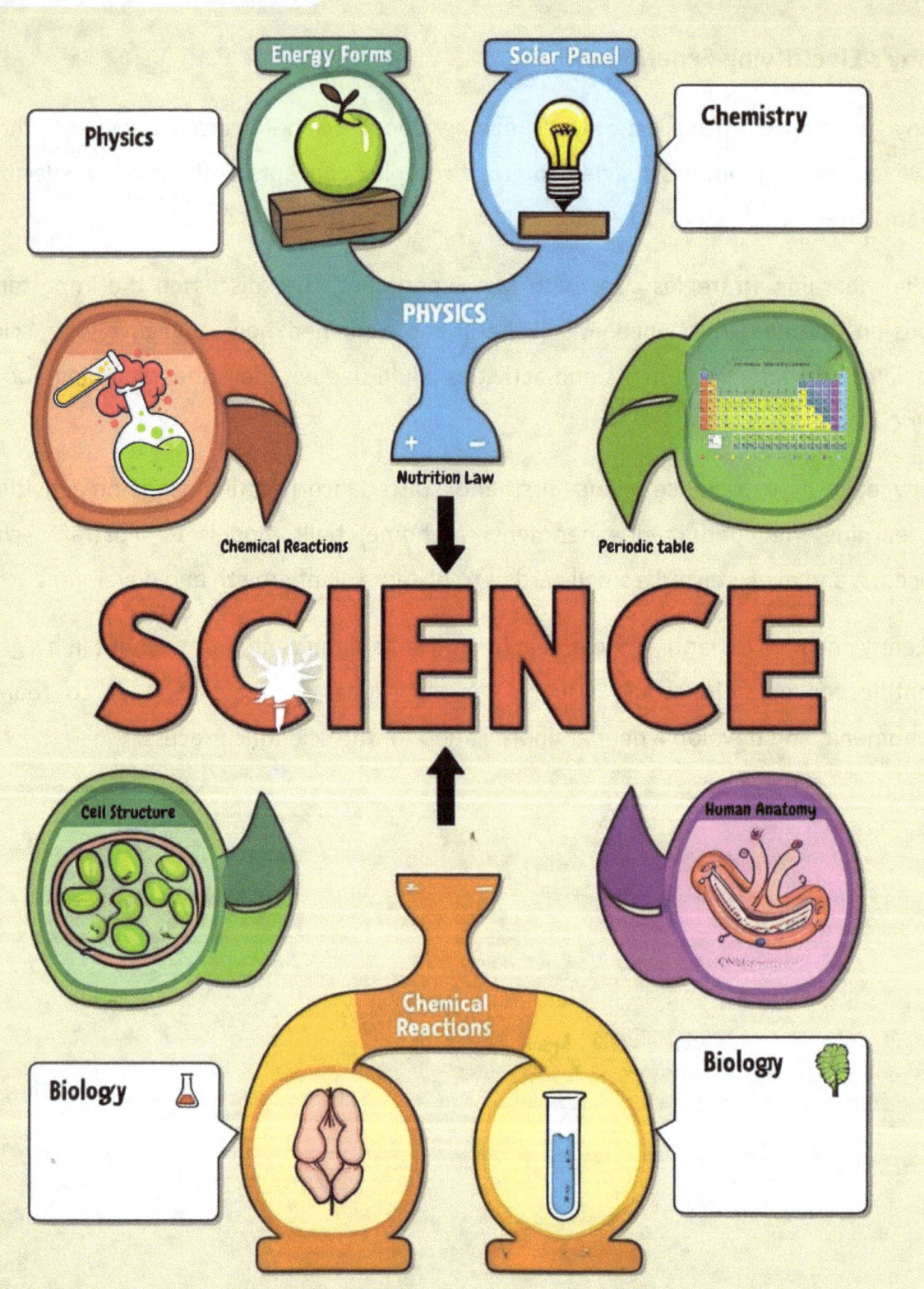

Lesson 2:
Concept Mapping

Mason's Musical Connections to Science

Mason, a talented musician, often saw science and music as separate disciplines. However, in their learning strategies class with Mr. Connect, they explored the interconnectedness of different subjects and the power of concept mapping to visualize relationships between ideas.

Mr. Connect explained how concept mapping could help them organize information, identify connections between concepts, and deepen their understanding of complex topics.

Mason, intrigued by this approach, started using concept maps to explore scientific concepts. He created maps to illustrate the relationships between different elements in the periodic table, the processes involved in the water cycle, and the connections between different musical notes and frequencies.

As Mason used concept maps to visualize scientific ideas, he discovered new connections and deepened his understanding of both science and music. He realized that seemingly disparate subjects could be interconnected and that exploring these relationships could enrich his learning experience.

Week 27: Science Strategies Continued

Introduction to Week 27

We're concluding our exploration of science strategies this week, focusing on how to think like true scientists. We'll delve into the process of scientific inquiry, sharpen our critical thinking skills, and discover how to apply our scientific knowledge to solve real-world problems. Get ready to put on your scientist hats and make a difference!

Lesson 1:
Scientific Inquiry and Critical Thinking

Nilan's Sports Science Investigation

Nilan, a sports enthusiast, loved playing and watching sports. However, he hadn't considered the science behind athletic performance until their learning strategies class with Mr. Inquiry.

Mr. Inquiry explained how scientific inquiry and critical thinking skills could be applied to analyze sports techniques, optimize training strategies, and understand the factors that contribute to athletic success.

Nilan, intrigued by this perspective, started applying his newfound knowledge to his favorite sport, basketball. He began observing professional players, analyzing their movements and techniques. He researched the biomechanics of shooting, the physics of ball trajectory, and the physiological factors that influence endurance and agility.

As Nilan applied scientific inquiry and critical thinking to his sports analysis, he gained a deeper appreciation for the complexities of athletic performance. He started experimenting with different shooting techniques, adjusting his training routine based on scientific principles, and even analyzing game statistics to identify areas for improvement.

Lesson 2: Applying Science to Real-World Problems

Lesson 2:
Applying Science to Real-World Problems

Naudia's Environmental Action Plan

Naudia, an empathetic student with a strong sense of justice, was concerned about environmental issues affecting her community. In their learning strategies class with Ms. Solution, they discussed how scientific knowledge could be applied to address real-world problems.

Ms. Solution explained how scientific principles could be used to develop sustainable solutions, conserve resources, and protect the environment.

Naudia, inspired to make a difference, started researching environmental issues in her community. She learned about water pollution, deforestation, and the impact of climate change. She also investigated sustainable practices, such as recycling, composting, and conserving energy.

Armed with this knowledge, Naudia developed an action plan to address environmental problems in her school and community. She organized a recycling campaign, initiated a composting project in the school garden, and presented her findings and recommendations to the local city council.

Unit 6:

Applying Superpowers to Social Skills and Conflict Resolution

Introduction to Unit 6

Our journey through the realm of superpowers has taken us through mindfulness, executive functioning, good habits, and academic strategies. Now, we're turning our attention to the incredible power of social skills and conflict resolution. Just as superheroes use their abilities to navigate complex situations and build strong alliances, we'll learn how to harness our superpowers to communicate effectively, build empathy, and resolve conflicts peacefully. Get ready to become social superheroes!

Week 28: Social Skills

Introduction to Week 28

Social skills are the superpowers that help us connect with others, build meaningful relationships, and navigate the social world with confidence. This week, we'll explore essential communication skills and discover how to cultivate empathy, the ability to understand and share the feelings of others. Get ready to unlock your social superpowers!

Lesson 1: Communication Skills

Nia's Communication Quest

Nia, a social butterfly, loved interacting with people and making new friends. However, she sometimes struggled to communicate her thoughts and feelings effectively. She had a habit of interrupting others, dominating conversations, and misinterpreting social cues.

In their learning strategies class with Mr. Communicate, they discussed the importance of effective communication skills in building strong relationships and navigating social situations with grace. Mr. Communicate emphasized the power of active listening, clear expression, and nonverbal communication.

Nia, eager to improve her communication skills, started practicing active listening techniques, paying close attention to what others were saying and asking clarifying questions. She also worked on expressing her thoughts and feelings clearly and respectfully, using "I" statements and considering the perspectives of others.

As Nia practiced these communication skills, she noticed a positive change in her interactions with others. She felt more confident expressing herself, and her relationships deepened as she learned to communicate with greater empathy and understanding.

Lesson 2: Building Empathy

Kenlyn's Empathetic Journey

Kenlyn, a peacemaker, always strived to understand others and resolve conflicts peacefully. However, she sometimes struggled to truly grasp the perspectives and emotions of those involved in disagreements.

In their learning strategies class with Ms. Empathy, they explored the concept of empathy and its importance in building strong relationships and resolving conflicts effectively. Ms. Empathy explained how empathy involves understanding and sharing the feelings of others, even if we don't agree with their actions or perspectives.

Kenlyn, eager to cultivate empathy, started practicing perspective-taking techniques. She began actively listening to others, asking questions to understand their viewpoints, and imagining herself in their shoes. She also started reading books and watching movies that portrayed diverse characters and experiences, expanding her understanding of different perspectives.

As Kenlyn practiced empathy, she noticed a shift in her interactions with others. She felt more compassionate and understanding, even when faced with challenging situations. She could approach conflicts with greater sensitivity and find solutions that addressed the needs of everyone involved.

Week 29: Social Skills Continued

Introduction to Week 29

We're continuing our exploration of social superpowers this week, diving deeper into the art of communication. We'll refine our active listening skills, learning to truly hear and understand others. We'll also explore the fascinating world of nonverbal communication, discovering how body language, facial expressions, and tone of voice can speak volumes. Get ready to become communication masters!

Lesson 1: Active Listening

Mason's Symphony of Listening

Mason, a talented musician, was accustomed to expressing himself through music. However, he sometimes struggled to truly listen to others, often getting caught up in his own thoughts and ideas.

In their learning strategies class with Ms. Attentive, they delved deeper into the power of active listening. Ms. Attentive explained how active listening involves not just hearing words but also paying attention to nonverbal cues, asking clarifying questions, and reflecting on the speaker's message.

Mason, inspired to become a better listener, started practicing these techniques in his interactions with others. He focused on making eye contact, nodding to show understanding, and summarizing the speaker's points to ensure he grasped their message accurately. He also started asking open-ended questions to encourage others to share their thoughts and feelings more fully.

As Mason honed his active listening skills, he noticed a significant improvement in his relationships. He felt more connected to others, and his conversations became more meaningful and fulfilling. He discovered that truly listening to others was like tuning into a beautiful symphony, each person's voice contributing to a harmonious whole.

Lesson 2: Nonverbal Communication

258

Lesson 2: Nonverbal Communication

Ahlani's Expressive Exploration

Ahlani, a history enthusiast, loved learning about different cultures and communication styles. However, she sometimes struggled to interpret nonverbal cues, which occasionally led to misunderstandings in her interactions with others.

In their learning strategies class with Ms. Expression, they explored the fascinating world of nonverbal communication. Ms. Expression explained how body language, facial expressions, and tone of voice could convey emotions, intentions, and attitudes.

Ahlani, eager to improve her understanding of nonverbal communication, started paying closer attention to these subtle cues in her interactions with others. She observed how people's posture, gestures, and facial expressions could convey confidence, nervousness, or even disagreement. She also noticed how tone of voice could change the meaning of words, expressing enthusiasm, sarcasm, or concern.

As Ahlani became more attuned to nonverbal communication, she felt more confident navigating social situations. She could better understand the unspoken messages conveyed by others and adjust her own communication style accordingly.

Week 30:
Conflict Resolution

Introduction to Week 30

Conflict is a natural part of life, but it doesn't have to be destructive. This week, we'll explore how our superpowers can help us navigate conflicts constructively and find peaceful solutions. We'll learn problem-solving steps to address disagreements effectively and discover how to regulate our emotions during challenging interactions. Get ready to become conflict resolution superheroes!

Lesson 1: Problem-Solving Steps

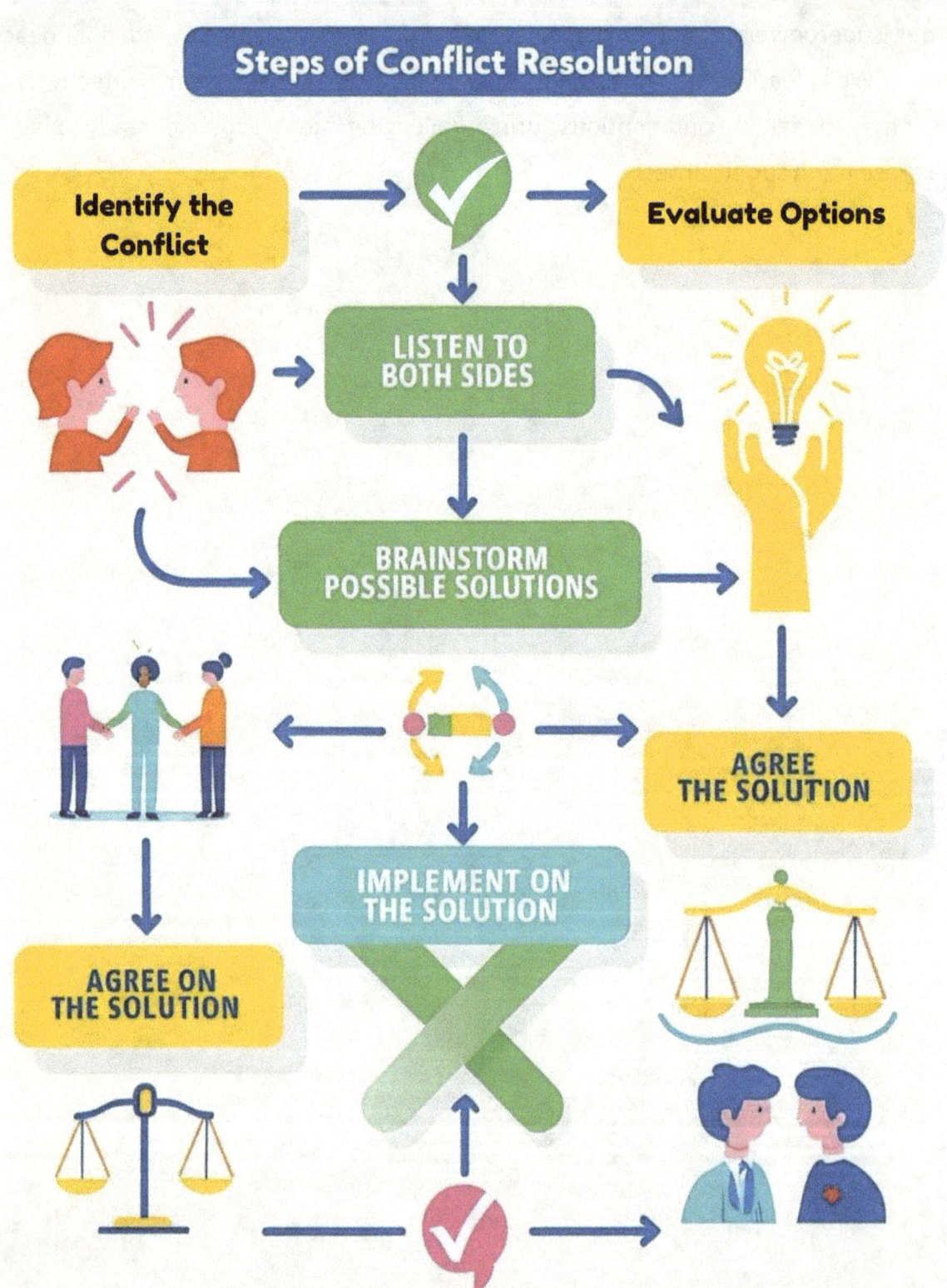

Lesson 1: Problem-Solving Steps

Naudia's Peaceful Playground

Naudia, an empathetic student, always tried to avoid conflicts. However, she realized that disagreements were inevitable, even in the friendliest environments like the playground.

One day, a dispute arose over who got to use the swing set first. Voices grew louder, and frustration filled the air. Naudia, remembering her learning strategies class with Mr. Resolve, decided to step in.

Mr. Resolve had taught them a powerful set of problem-solving steps:

1. **Identify the Problem:** Clearly define the issue at hand.

2. **Brainstorm Solutions:** Generate multiple possible solutions without judgment.

3. **Evaluate Solutions:** Assess the pros and cons of each solution.

4. **Choose a Solution:** Select the solution that seems most fair and effective.

5. **Implement and Evaluate:** Put the solution into action and assess its effectiveness.

Naudia calmly facilitated a discussion, guiding her classmates through these steps. They identified the problem (limited swings, high demand), brainstormed solutions (taking turns, using other equipment, creating a schedule), and evaluated each option. Finally, they agreed on a fair solution: a timed rotation system for the swings.

Lesson 2:
Emotional Regulation in Conflict

Nyrie's Calm Canvas

Nyrie, a creative artist, often felt overwhelmed by strong emotions during conflicts. He had a habit of reacting impulsively, which sometimes escalated disagreements and created hurt feelings.

In their learning strategies class with Ms. Harmony, they explored the importance of emotional regulation in conflict resolution. Ms. Harmony explained how recognizing and managing emotions could help them respond to conflicts more constructively.

Nyrie, determined to improve his emotional regulation, started practicing mindfulness techniques. He learned to take deep breaths when feeling overwhelmed, to label his emotions, and to express his feelings calmly and respectfully. He also discovered that engaging in creative activities, like painting or drawing, helped him channel his emotions and find inner peace during challenging situations.

As Nyrie practiced emotional regulation, he noticed a significant difference in his ability to navigate conflicts. He felt more in control of his reactions, and his interactions with others became more positive and productive.

Week 31: Conflict Resolution Continued

Introduction to Week 31

We're continuing our journey through the realm of conflict resolution this week, focusing on how to communicate effectively during disagreements and find common ground to build bridges instead of walls. Just as superheroes use their communication skills to de-escalate tense situations and forge alliances, we'll learn how to express ourselves clearly, listen with empathy, and discover shared interests that can lead to peaceful resolutions.

Lesson 1:
Effective Communication in Conflicts

Levi's Digital Diplomacy

Levi, a tech-savvy student, was comfortable communicating online, where he could carefully craft his messages and avoid face-to-face confrontations. However, he sometimes struggled to express himself effectively during in-person conflicts, often resorting to sarcasm or withdrawing from the conversation altogether.

In their learning strategies class with Ms. Dialogue, they explored the nuances of effective communication in conflict resolution. Ms. Dialogue emphasized the importance of using "I" statements, active listening, and respectful language, even when emotions run high.

Levi, determined to improve his communication skills, started practicing these techniques in real-life situations. He began using "I" statements to express his feelings and needs without blaming others. He focused on actively listening to understand the perspectives of those involved in the conflict. He also made a conscious effort to use respectful language, even when he felt frustrated or disagreed with others' viewpoints.

As Levi practiced these communication strategies, he noticed a positive shift in his ability to navigate conflicts. He felt more confident expressing himself, and his interactions became more productive and less likely to escalate into arguments. He discovered that effective communication was a powerful tool for building understanding and finding common ground.

Lesson 2: Finding Common Ground

Lesson 2:
Finding Common Ground

Noah's Collaborative Creation

Noah, a budding inventor, loved working on his own projects and coming up with unique solutions. However, he sometimes struggled to collaborate with others, especially when their ideas differed from his own.

In their learning strategies class with Ms. Collaborate, they explored the importance of finding common ground in conflict resolution. Ms. Collaborate explained how identifying shared interests and goals could help bridge differences and foster cooperation.

Noah, eager to improve his collaboration skills, started practicing active listening and perspective-taking during group projects. He made a conscious effort to understand his classmates' ideas, even if they initially seemed different from his own. He also started looking for ways to combine or adapt ideas to create solutions that incorporated everyone's contributions.

As Noah practiced finding common ground, he discovered that collaboration could lead to more creative and innovative solutions than working alone. He learned to appreciate the diverse perspectives of his classmates and realized that working together could be a rewarding and enriching experience.

Week 32: Integrating Social Skills and Conflict Resolution

Introduction to Week 32

We've explored a range of social skills and conflict resolution strategies, from active listening to finding common ground. This week, we'll focus on integrating these superpowers into our daily lives, practicing them in various situations and solidifying our ability to navigate the social world with confidence and compassion.

Lesson 1: Social Skills in Daily Life

Lesson 1:
Social Skills in Daily Life

Kimiyah's Kindness Campaign

Kimiyah, a determined learner, was always focused on achieving her goals. However, she sometimes overlooked the importance of social connections and the power of kindness in building positive relationships.

In their learning strategies class with Mr. Connect, they discussed how social skills could enhance their daily lives, creating a more positive and supportive environment for themselves and others. Mr. Connect emphasized the importance of kindness, empathy, and respect in all their interactions.

Kimiyah, inspired to make a difference, decided to launch a "Kindness Campaign" in her school. She started by practicing small acts of kindness, such as offering compliments, helping others, and expressing gratitude. She also encouraged her classmates to participate, creating a ripple effect of positivity throughout the school.

As Kimiyah integrated social skills into her daily life, she noticed a transformation in her relationships and her overall well-being. She felt more connected to her peers, and her school environment became more welcoming and supportive. She discovered that kindness was a superpower that could brighten everyone's day and create a more harmonious world.

Lesson 2:
Conflict Resolution Practice

Nilan's Team Spirit

Nilan, a sports enthusiast, loved the thrill of competition. However, he sometimes struggled to handle disagreements within his team, letting his competitive spirit escalate into arguments.

In their learning strategies class with Ms. Teamwork, they practiced applying conflict resolution strategies in various team-based activities and challenges. Ms. Teamwork emphasized the importance of communication, compromise, and respecting diverse perspectives to achieve shared goals.

Nilan, determined to improve his teamwork skills, started applying the conflict resolution strategies he had learned. He practiced active listening to understand his teammates' perspectives, expressed his own needs and concerns clearly, and looked for solutions that benefited the entire team.

As Nilan practiced conflict resolution within his team, he noticed a positive shift in their dynamics. They became more collaborative, supportive, and successful in achieving their goals. He discovered that resolving conflicts constructively could strengthen team bonds and enhance their collective performance.

Week 33: Reflection and Growth

Introduction to Week 33

We've reached the final week of our superpower journey! This week, we'll take time to reflect on our incredible growth and celebrate the amazing progress we've made. We'll look back on our social skills development, our conflict resolution triumphs, and the valuable lessons we've learned along the way.

Lesson 1: Reflecting on Social Skills Development

Lesson 1:
Reflecting on Social Skills Development

Ahlani's Social Skills Showcase

Ahlani, a history enthusiast, used to be shy and reserved in social situations. However, throughout this unit, she had blossomed into a confident and empathetic communicator.

In their learning strategies class with Mr. Celebrate, they reflected on their social skills development journey. Mr. Celebrate encouraged them to acknowledge their progress, celebrate their achievements, and identify areas for continued growth.

Ahlani, proud of her transformation, shared how she had overcome her shyness, improved her communication skills, and learned to build strong relationships based on kindness and understanding. She also acknowledged that social skills are an ongoing journey and that she would continue to practice and refine her abilities.

Lesson 2:
Reflecting on Conflict Resolution Growth

Naudia's Peaceful Resolution Reflection

Naudia, an empathetic student, had always valued peace and harmony. However, she used to shy away from conflicts, fearing that disagreements would damage relationships.

In their learning strategies class with Ms. Reflect, they looked back on their conflict resolution journey. Ms. Reflect encouraged them to acknowledge their growth, celebrate their successes, and identify areas where they could continue to hone their conflict resolution skills.

Naudia, proud of her progress, shared how she had learned to approach conflicts constructively, using effective communication and problem-solving strategies to find peaceful resolutions. She also acknowledged that conflict resolution is an ongoing process and that she would continue to practice and refine her skills to navigate disagreements with grace and understanding.

Unit 7:
Putting It All Together

Introduction to Unit 7

Congratulations! You've journeyed through the exciting world of superpowers, mastering mindfulness, executive functioning, good habits, academic strategies, social skills, and conflict resolution. Now, it's time to put it all together, integrating these powerful tools into a cohesive whole and applying them to real-world situations. Get ready to unleash your full potential and become a true superhero in all aspects of your life!

Week 34: Combining Superpowers

Introduction to Week 34

This week, we'll focus on integrating the various superpowers we've developed, creating a synergistic blend of skills and strategies that will empower us to navigate any challenge with confidence and grace.

Lesson 1: Integrating Meditation, Executive Functioning, and Good Habits

Lesson 1: Integrating Meditation, Executive Functioning, and Good Habits

The Superhero Summit

Imagine a grand summit where all the superheroes we've met throughout this journey gather to share their wisdom and combine their powers. Mindful Mason, Organized Noah, Focused Nyrie, Communicative Nia, Empathetic Naudia, and all the others come together, ready to create a master plan for success.

They discuss how meditation can enhance focus and emotional regulation, how executive functioning skills can improve organization and planning, and how good habits can create a foundation for consistent growth. They realize that these superpowers work best when combined, creating a synergistic force that amplifies their individual strengths.

Inspired by this collaboration, they create a "Superpower Integration Plan," outlining how they will incorporate these skills into their daily lives. They commit to practicing mindfulness regularly, utilizing executive functioning strategies to tackle tasks effectively, and cultivating good habits that support their overall well-being.

Lesson 2: Personal Growth Reflection

Lesson 2: Personal Growth Reflection

The Hero's Journey

Every superhero embarks on a hero's journey, facing challenges, overcoming obstacles, and emerging transformed. As we reach the culmination of our superpower program, it's time to reflect on our own hero's journey.

We've learned to quiet our minds, focus our attention, organize our thoughts, regulate our emotions, build positive habits, communicate effectively, resolve conflicts peacefully, and apply our skills to academic and real-world challenges.

We've discovered that our superpowers are not just skills; they are qualities that reside within us, waiting to be unleashed. We've learned that we have the power to shape our own destinies, to overcome adversity, and to create a positive impact on the world around us.

Week 35: Practical Application

Introduction to Week 35

We've integrated our superpowers and reflected on our growth. Now, it's time to put our skills to the test in real-world scenarios and celebrate our incredible achievements!

Lesson 1:
Real-World Scenarios

The Community Challenge

The superheroes from our learning strategies class decide to put their combined powers to good use by tackling a real-world challenge in their community. They identify a local issue, such as environmental conservation, supporting a local charity, or promoting inclusivity and kindness.

They apply their mindfulness, executive functioning skills, and good habits to plan and execute a project that addresses this challenge. They communicate effectively, collaborate with others, and navigate any conflicts that arise with grace and understanding.

Through their combined efforts, they make a positive impact on their community, demonstrating the power of their superpowers to create real-world change.

Lesson 2: Celebration of Achievements

Lesson 2:
Celebration of Achievements

The Superhero Celebration

The superheroes from our learning strategies class gather for a grand celebration, commemorating their incredible journey and acknowledging their remarkable achievements.

They share stories of their triumphs, expressing gratitude for the support they've received and the lessons they've learned. They celebrate their individual growth and the collective power they've harnessed throughout the program.

They recognize that their superpower journey doesn't end here; it's an ongoing adventure filled with opportunities to learn, grow, and make a positive impact on the world.

Unit 8:

Maintaining and Sustaining Growth

Introduction to Unit 8

Congratulations on completing the Superpower Program! You've developed an incredible set of skills and strategies to navigate life's challenges with confidence and grace. This final unit focuses on maintaining and sustaining your growth, ensuring that your superpowers continue to empower you on your lifelong journey.

Week 36: Sustaining Practices

Introduction to Week 36

This week, we'll explore how to sustain the practices that have fueled your growth, setting long-term goals and embracing continuous improvement as a way of life.

Lesson 1: Long-Term Goal Setting

Lesson 1: Long-Term Goal Setting

The Superhero's Legacy

Every superhero leaves a legacy, inspiring others and making a lasting impact on the world. As we conclude our superpower journey, it's time to consider our own legacy and set long-term goals that align with our values and aspirations.

We've learned that growth is an ongoing process, and our superpowers can continue to evolve and expand as we pursue our dreams and make a positive difference in the world.

Lesson 2:
Continuous Improvement

The Ever-Evolving Hero

Superheroes never stop learning and growing. They embrace challenges as opportunities for improvement, constantly refining their skills and adapting to new situations.

As we conclude our superpower program, we recognize that our journey doesn't end here. We are all "ever-evolving heroes," committed to continuous improvement and lifelong learning.

Tab 1

Surveys

Pre and Post Surveys

These pre- and post-surveys help students reflect on their growth and development throughout each unit. They also provide valuable feedback for teachers to ensure that the curriculum effectively meets the students' needs.

Unit 1:
I Am Unique – Discovering Who I Am and Unleashing My Powers

Pre-Survey

1. How would you describe your unique strengths?

2. What are some challenges you face in your learning process?

3. How do you feel about being different from your peers?

4. What strategies do you currently use to overcome your challenges?

5. On a scale of 1-10, how confident do you feel about your abilities?

Post-Survey

1. How has your understanding of your unique strengths changed after this unit?

2. What new strategies have you learned to overcome your challenges?

3. How do you feel about your differences now compared to before this unit?

4. Describe a moment from this unit that helped you feel more confident about your abilities.

5. On a scale of 1-10, how confident do you feel about your abilities?

Unit 2:
The Superpower of Meditation

Pre-Survey

1. Have you ever practiced meditation before? If so, how often?

2. How do you currently manage stress and anxiety?

3. What are your expectations from learning meditation?

4. On a scale of 1-10, how well do you focus during study sessions?

5. How do you feel about your current ability to manage emotions?

Post-Survey

1. How has practicing meditation affected your stress levels?

2. Describe how meditation has impacted your focus during study sessions.

3. What meditation techniques did you find most helpful?

4. On a scale of 1-10, how well do you focus during study sessions now?

5. How do you feel about your ability to manage emotions after completing this unit?

Unit 3:
The Superpower of Executive Functioning Skills

Pre-Survey

1. How do you currently plan and organize your schoolwork?

2. What challenges do you face with time management?

3. How do you approach problem-solving in your academic tasks?

4. On a scale of 1-10, how effectively do you use your memory in learning?

5. What are your goals for improving your executive functioning skills?

Post-Survey

1. How have your planning and organizational skills improved after this unit?

2. Describe any changes in your time management practices.

3. What new problem-solving strategies have you learned?

4. On a scale of 1-10, how effectively do you use your memory in learning now?

5. How have you progressed toward your goals for executive functioning skills?

Unit 4:
The Superpower of Good Habits

Pre-Survey

1. What good habits do you currently practice in your daily routine?

2. What bad habits would you like to change?

3. How consistent are you with your habits? (Rate 1-10)

4. What challenges do you face in maintaining good habits?

5. What do you hope to achieve by developing better habits?

Post-Survey

1. What new good habits have you developed through this unit?

2. How have you addressed and changed any bad habits?

3. How consistent are you with your habits now? (Rate 1-10)

4. Describe any strategies that helped you maintain good habits.

5. How has developing better habits impacted your daily routine?

Unit 5:
Applying Superpowers to Academics

Pre-Survey

1. Which academic subjects do you find most challenging?

2. How do you currently approach studying for these subjects?

3. What strategies do you use to improve your academic performance?

4. On a scale of 1-10, how confident do you feel about your academic abilities?

5. What are your academic goals for this unit?

Post-Survey

1. How has this unit helped you with your most challenging subjects?

2. Describe any new study approaches you have adopted.

3. What strategies from this unit have improved your academic performance?

4. On a scale of 1-10, how confident do you feel about your academic abilities?

5. How have you progressed toward your academic goals?

Unit 6:
Applying Superpowers to Social Skills and Conflict Resolution

Pre-Survey

1. How would you describe your current social skills?

2. What challenges do you face in social interactions?

3. How do you typically resolve conflicts?

4. On a scale of 1-10, how comfortable are you in social situations?

5. What do you hope to achieve regarding social skills and conflict resolution in this unit?

Post-Survey

1. How have your social skills improved after this unit?

2. Describe any strategies you have learned to overcome social challenges.

3. How has your approach to resolving conflicts changed?

4. On a scale of 1-10, how comfortable are you in social situations now?

5. How have you progressed toward your goals in social skills and conflict resolution?

Unit 7:
Putting It All Together

Pre-Survey

1. **On a scale of 1-5 (1 being not at all confident, 5 being very confident), how confident are you in your ability to use meditation to improve your focus and concentration?**

    - 1 2 3 4 5

2. **How often do you use executive functioning skills (planning, organization, time management) in your daily life?**

    - Never Rarely Sometimes Often Very Often

3. **How consistent are you in practicing positive habits that support your well-being and success?**

    - Not at all consistent Slightly consistent Moderately consistent Mostly consistent Very consistent

4. **How comfortable are you applying the skills you've learned (meditation, executive functioning, good habits) to real-life situations and challenges?**

    - Not at all comfortable Slightly comfortable Moderately comfortable Mostly comfortable Very comfortable

5. **What are your biggest challenges when it comes to integrating these skills and applying them to your life?** (Open-ended response)

Post-Survey

1. **After completing Unit 7, how has your confidence in using meditation to improve your focus and concentration changed?**

    - Increased significantly Increased slightly Stayed the same Decreased slightly Decreased significantly

2. **How frequently are you now using executive functioning skills in your daily life compared to before Unit 7?**

    - More frequently Slightly more frequently About the same Slightly less frequently Less frequently

3. **How has your consistency in practicing positive habits changed since completing Unit 7?**

    - More consistent Slightly more consistent About the same Slightly less consistent Less consistent

4. **How comfortable do you now feel applying the skills you've learned to real-life situations and challenges?**

    - More comfortable Slightly more comfortable About the same Slightly less comfortable Less comfortable

5. **What specific benefits have you experienced from integrating and applying these skills to your life?** (Open-ended response)

Unit 8:
Maintaining and Sustaining Growth

Pre-Survey

1. **On a scale of 1-5 (1 being not at all important, 5 being very important), how important is it to you to continue growing and developing your skills throughout your life?**

   - 1 2 3 4 5

2. **How confident are you in your ability to set and achieve long-term goals?**

   - Not at all confident Slightly confident Moderately confident Mostly confident Very confident

3. **How often do you reflect on your progress and make adjustments to your goals and strategies?**

   - Never Rarely Sometimes Often Very often

4. **How comfortable are you seeking feedback from others to support your growth and development?**

   - Not at all comfortable Slightly comfortable Moderately comfortable Mostly comfortable Very comfortable

5. **What are your biggest challenges when it comes to maintaining and sustaining your personal growth?** (Open-ended response)

Post-Survey

1. **After completing Unit 8, how has your perspective on the importance of lifelong growth and development changed?**

    - More important Slightly more important About the same Slightly less important Less important

2. **How confident do you now feel in your ability to set and achieve long-term goals?**

    - More confident Slightly more confident About the same Slightly less confident Less confident

3. **How often do you now reflect on your progress and make adjustments to your goals and strategies?**

    - More often Slightly more often About the same Slightly less often Less often

4. **How comfortable do you now feel seeking feedback from others to support your growth?**

    - More comfortable Slightly more comfortable About the same Slightly less comfortable Less comfortable

5. **What specific strategies or resources have you found most helpful for maintaining and sustaining your personal growth?** (Open-ended response)

Additional Resources:

Books:

Meditation:

- Mindfulness for Teen Anxiety: A Workbook to Help You Deal with Stress, Worry, and Panic by Dr. Christopher Willard
- The Relaxation and Stress Reduction Workbook for Teens: Mindfulness Skills to Help You Deal with Stress, Anxiety, and Depression by Dr. Christopher Willard
- A Still Quiet Place for Teens: A Mindfulness Workbook for Learning to Live in the Moment by Amy Saltzman

Executive Functioning:

- Learning to Learn: How to Study Smarter, Not Harder by Barbara Oakley (Offers practical study strategies and explains how the brain learns)
- The Teenage Brain: A Neuroscientist's Survival Guide to Raising Adolescents and Young Adults by Frances E. Jensen (Explains the science of the teenage brain in an accessible way)

Habits:

- The 7 Habits of Highly Effective Teens by Sean Covey
- Better Than Before: Mastering the Habits of Our Everyday Lives by Gretchen Rubin (While written for adults, many of the concepts are applicable to teens)

Websites:

- Khan Academy: www.khanacademy.org (Offers free lessons and practice exercises in various subjects, including math and science)
- How to ADHD: www.howtoadhd.com (A YouTube channel and website with helpful tips and strategies for managing ADHD, including executive functioning challenges)
- Teen Breathe Magazine: www.teenbreathe.co.uk (A magazine and website with articles and resources on mindfulness, well-being, and personal growth for teenagers)

Meet the Author

Alisa Ladawn Grace is a seasoned educator, transformative life coach, and local missionary with over 30 years of experience serving her community. Her unwavering commitment to expressing, displaying, and demonstrating unconditional love has made her a beacon of hope in a world often marred by division, strife, and discord. Alisa's passion for helping others through love is the foundation of her life's work, inspiring individuals to thrive and reach their full potential.

Alisa holds a Specialist degree in Curriculum and Instruction and brings over two decades of experience in Exceptional Student Education, Reading Coaching, Instructional Coaching, and school administration. Her tenure as Chief Operating Officer of a non-profit organization further honed her leadership and strategic planning skills, making her a dynamic force in education and personal development.

Her dedication to empowering the next generation extends to her authorship of several impactful works. Alisa is the author of *Civic Heroes: Discovering Elections with the Supervisor of Elections*, *My Civic Adventure: Learning About Voting and Community!*, and *Unlocking Your Great Potential Within You: A Comprehensive Guide to Nurturing Children's Mindfulness, Executive Functioning, and Positive Habits*. These books reflect her passion for civic engagement and holistic development, making complex ideas accessible and inspiring for young minds.

Alisa's most recent work, *Love's Unconditional Revolution! Unleash and Ignite the Transformative Power of Love: Unlocking the Limitless Potential of 1 Corinthians 13:4-7*, is a guide to applying the practical principles of love to every aspect of life. From relationships to personal growth, this book empowers readers to harness the transformative power of love and create positive change in their lives.

Her dedication to love and education converges in her groundbreaking curriculum, **Unlocking Your Great Potential Within You Using the Superpowers of Meditation, Executive Functioning Skills, and Good Habits, We Can Do It!**. This comprehensive program equips middle and high school students with disabilities with the tools to thrive academically, socially, and emotionally.

By integrating meditation, executive functioning skills, and good habits into a cohesive framework, Alisa continues her mission to inspire and uplift others. Her work reflects her deep belief in the power of love and the potential within every individual to overcome challenges and achieve greatness.

Join Alisa Ladawn Grace on this transformative journey and discover how to unlock your own potential while fostering hope and love in the world around you.

www.ingramcontent.com/pod-product-compliance
Lightning Source LLC
Chambersburg PA
CBHW082226010526
44111CB00040BA/2893